HISTORIC HAUNTS
of the
SOUTH

JAMIE ROUSH PEARCE

THE SECOND BOOK IN THE
HISTORIC HAUNTS SERIES

D1472294

Inquiries should be addressed to:
Jamie Roush Pearce
historichaunts@yahoo.com

HISTORIC HAUNTS SERIES:
Historic Haunts Florida
Historic Haunts *of the* South

Foreward:
In this book I tried to include any and all personal experiences I had at each of the locations I've written about. Unfortunately, ghosts, as I like to say, do not perform on cue. In situations where my personal experiences were limited, I tried to interview people who lived or worked at the locations, past or present. Hours of research, traveling to the different locations, visiting, investigating, touring, and interviewing, all went into writing this book and I loved every moment of it! I have heard a lot of fascinating stories, experienced a lot of paranormal activity, and have made new friends. The trouble with putting this book together was not how to find and investigate places in the South, but how many I could squeeze into one book! I covered a lot, but also left a lot out, I soon realized I would need to write another. So be on the lookout for part II, where I hope to make it up to those states and places I may have excluded.

Dedication:
To my amazing husband, Deric. You have made my life complete, without you I wouldn't be the person I am today. Your love and support have made me happier and stronger than I ever could have dreamed. Thank you from the bottom of my heart! <3 XOX,
Jamie

Special Thanks:
Assistant Investigator: Gayel Roush

Editing: Deric Pearce & Paula Dillon

Design and Layout: Deric Pearce
All images unless otherwise credited are provided courtesy of the author
Additional photography provided by and copyright Big Stock

Second Printing April 2014
ISBN: 978-1492266549

HISTORIC HAUNTS OF THE SOUTH

Table of Contents

4

THE HAUNTED WINDOW
Pickens County Courthouse, Carrollton, Alabama

They say that the eyes are the windows to the soul. What if you could capture an image of those eyes, and perhaps that soul for posterity, indelibly etched long after its passing? Many believe that this has happened several times, to a select group of unlucky souls. Some believe that with a little help from circumstance (and Mother Nature) these select few have left a lasting impression on the world of the living long after their passing. The most renowned of these cases occurred at Pickens County Courthouse in Carrolton, Alabama.

Photo courtesy of Wikimedia Commons and the United States Department of Agriculture

The Legends behind the Haunted Courthouse

The first Pickens County Courthouse was burnt down by Union Troops during the Civil War and a new one was rebuilt shortly thereafter. The town had little money or supplies to accomplish this, but with hard work and sacrifice the town was somehow able to get the project done. Unfortunately, less than 12 years after the first courthouse was burnt to the ground, the second one went up in flames. The people of Carrollton could only watch in disbelief as the courthouse became a pile of charred rubble.

The angry townspeople wanted to know the culprit's reasons and why their courthouse was gone. They learned that the fire was apparently caused by a burglary that had gone wrong. The townspeople suspected a freed slave who lived close, named Henry Wells, and might be responsible. Stories around town about Wells were already bad (as was his reputation). He was known to have a major temper, he carried a straight razor, and he had been involved in many fights throughout the county.

In 1878, Henry Wells was formally accused of burning down the courthouse that was a source of pride for Carrollton County. Despite the existence of only vague circumstantial evidence against Wells, he was arrested and charged with burglary, arson, assault with intent to kill, and carrying a concealed weapon.

The Sheriff, a very astute man, had a bad feeling about what was to come as word spread about Wells' arrest. Concerned, he took Wells to the new courthouse (1877) and told him to lay low and keep quiet.

5

As the crowd gathered and became more irate Wells got scared and curious as to what was going on outside so he stood up to look out the window. He saw the mob in a fit of rage and shouted out to them, "I am innocent. If you kill me, I am going to haunt you for the rest of your lives." Just as Wells finished proclaiming his innocence a bolt of lightning struck the building revealing Wells' fearful face to the mob.

The angry lynch mob (made up in some cases of drunkards and troublemakers) broke into the courthouse and dragged Wells outside. They did away with him as he continued to plead his innocence. At the time no thought was given to the accused man's haunting threat that would soon change.

The next morning a hung over member of the previous night's mob was passing by the courthouse and looked up at the garret window where Wells had been the night before. There in the window, was an image of Henry Wells (believed to have been captured by the lightning that had struck the prior evening as the terrified Henry looked down and shouted to the crowd). The man was shocked and in disbelief that the image was there. He screamed to the other townspeople to come and look. They were all terrified when they saw the image permanently etched in the window and Wells' threat of coming back and haunting everyone now seemed real. Or so the legend goes...

The Real History behind the Legend

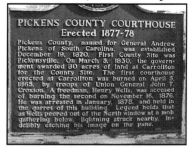

PICKENS COUNTY COURTHOUSE
Erected 1877-78

*Historical marker from the
Pickens County Courthouse
in Carrollton, Alabama.
courtesy Wikimedia Commons*

The Pickens County legend about Henry Wells' face and fate is apparently a mixture of two different local stories intertwined together. There was a lynch mob at the courthouse, but they were actually after Nathaniel Pierce, who was being held for murder. He was the one the mob was after and the victim of mob justice. Pierce had nothing to do with the courthouse being burned down. Wells, on the other hand, reportedly admitted to burning the 2nd courthouse down after being shot twice trying to escape from the cops.

There also seems to be some question about the windows themselves. Many believe there is no possible way that either of the men's faces are in the window. According to a report by a local newspaper, the 1877 courthouse didn't have garret windows installed until after both men were dead. However, the times and dates are very close and could have easily gotten confused. In fact, the courthouse reports the official date of death for Wells for later, after the windows were in place.

The Real and Surreal Details of the Haunted Window

Whether the windows were in place or not, the presence of an image in the window is irrefutable. The county has even erected an historical marker and indicators to visitors. The image is easily seen and depending on the angle viewed, appears more or less face like. Despite repeated efforts with solvents and scrubbing (among other things) to erase the image from the glass it still remains. The "haunted" image is only visible from outside the courthouse; from inside the courthouse it appears as a normal glass pane.

Oddly enough, this is not the first case of a lightning etched image in a window. Other examples have been reported and confirmed, including a naked bather in Russelville, Kentucky, a slave in Clay's Ferry, Kentucky and a prominent woman of Chennuggee Ridge, in the same state as the Pickens County Courthouse. Some speculate that x-rays from the lightning could have caused the images, and that perhaps these window panes had characteristics in common with the photographic glass plates used at the time. Other theories suggest oil from the skin or sweat worked in combination with the freak electrical storms to create the images.

Regardless of the scientific explanation for the phenomenon, the visitors to Pickens County Courthouse seem eager to learn whose face is in the window. Maybe Wells did return after his death as a reminder of his promise, if it was ever really made. Reports abound of those who have seen the ghost of Henry Wells while thunderstorms roll through Carrollton. His face and body appear to these eyewitnesses and appear to make this etched image even more unsettling. The jury is still out on whether this is a residual haunting from a long gone prisoner, or the paranormal energies of Henry Wells.

The story has garnered attention in local legends and several books of ghost stories. Interesting, and also difficult to explain is the fact that the building has been repeatedly hit by hailstorms, and that every pane has been broken by these storms at one time or another except the one believed to house Henry Wells' image. Perhaps this is a continuing example of Mother Nature herself shedding a little light on the wrongs of a lynch mob mentality. If you happen to visit during a stormy night, you may be shocked to learn the answers behind this Historic Haunt for yourself!

GHOSTS OF THE MIGHTY A
USS Alabama Battleship, Mobile, Alabama

There are many stories of the heroism and accomplishments of WWII's "greatest generation". Brave men and woman fought and died to keep our country free. Like their Revolutionary fore fathers their efforts should not be forgotten. Fortunately, we have monuments like the USS Alabama to help us remember. Sometimes, these ghosts of the past remind us in more direct ways.

The History of the Alabama

Building began on the USS Alabama Battleship in Norfolk Virginia in 1940. She was launched on February 16th, 1942. The Alabama was a South Dakota class battleship built for WWII and became known as the "Mighty A".

As one in a long line of vessels named "Alabama", she had a fighting name to live up to. The Alabama's first main Pacific engagement was in November and December 1943. It was at Gilbert Island where she made her way through to help plan the attack on Caroline and Mariana Islands. This beautiful battleship was credited for shooting down a total of 23 Japanese aircraft. She also bombarded many enemy installations, and was crucial in operations to free the Philippines and to provide support for Allied fleet and landing operations. She made it through WWII with no casualties or damage from enemy fire, and even, rode out a typhoon in June of 1945 suffering only minor damage. When WWII ended the USS Alabama returned close to 3,700 veterans to the United States. The Battleship was decommissioned on January 9th, 1947 and was brought to Mobile Bay in 1964.

Unfortunately, there were a few deaths connected to the Alabama. Before she was launched in February of 1942, two men died accidently during her construction at the Norfolk Naval Shipyard. In addition, Eight people in gun mount #5 were killed during friendly fire from another gun turret (gun mount #9) on the ship. The safety feature to keep the guns from firing failed. Mount #9 accidently fired a round into mount #5 which exploded and killed all who were inside. All that reportedly remained of the men was the grisly mess and the commander's boots.

Now, you can tour the battleship and learn more about the history of the battles she fought and the crew who served on her. You may also have an interesting experience while aboard, a paranormal experience to be exact.

The Alabama's Paranormal Activity

The loss of life on the ship, though not from battle, might explain the ghosts attached to the battleship and the paranormal activity encountered. Many people have reported seeing the construction workers who died during the unfortunate accident at the naval shipyards. They appear in 1940's era clothing and look like construction workers or handymen. Also, the report of tools dropping and hitting the floor can be heard in the belly of the ship. Further, there are also reports of the sounds of banging and hammering as if someone is still working on the construction of the ship.

Apparently there are a few soldiers still aboard as well. Men in military uniforms have been seen and voices have been heard. These apparitions also reportedly appear in 1940's era uniforms. In fact, the most common entity reported is that of a young blonde haired sailor frequently seen in the Officer's Quarters and the cook's galley. These spirits are typically encountered when someone has roamed off from their family or group. Despite these encounters no one has ever been harmed, but the activity has scared a few people. Many believe these may be the men who were killed in Mount #5 when the gun accidently fired.

In addition to the apparitions, there are several reports of other paranormal activity. Footsteps are often heard behind people, who turn around and discover they are very much alone. Heavy steel doors and airtight hatches on the superstructure reportedly open and slam shut on their own. Bulkheads seem to come alive with popping and tapping, and overnight guests aboard the ship report being chased by something unseen.

Overall, the Alabama is an amazing piece of history. Visitors can learn about this incredible vessel and the men who served their country aboard her. Men who, like the Alabama, should not be forgotten and may still be returning to remind us.

INMATES IN THE AFTERLIFE
Old Clay County Jail, Green Cove Springs, Florida

The Old Clay County Jail

What is your idea of a scary location? If you were to make a short list chances are it might include an old jail. And why not? The thought of being locked up and losing your freedom is scary enough, but what if there was something from the other side trapped in there with you? It would make for a pretty good movie and an amazing paranormal investigation. In this case it's not just theoretical, it's historical. It's the Old Clay County Jail.

History of a Jail

Nestled among the huge oak trees covered with Spanish moss in the heart of historic Green Cove Springs Florida is the Old Clay County Jail. It was constructed in 1894 and in operation until 1972. It is the second oldest jail in Florida (the oldest by a mere 3 years is the Old St. Johns County Jail - see Historic Haunts Florida). Today it is available for tours and investigations and hosts the Clay County Archives.

Built on land originally owned by the heir to the Borden Condensed Milk fortune; the structure was originally red brick with living space for jailors and their families, room for law enforcement operations, and cells in the rear. The facility was enlarged in the 1930's, to provide additional cells and expanded jailor's quarters. Even with the expansion and until its closing the Clay County Jail experienced the same problems of overcrowding, poor living conditions, and death and disease as many other jails. Before its current incarnation, and as the records and archives can confirm, it's seen a lot of drama and violence in its nearly 80 years.

There were at least five documented executions that took place on the front steps, all by hanging. At least one sheriff was assassinated here and his body was drug into the building where he bled out on the floor. The jail wasn't only used for housing male prisoners; it also housed women, juveniles, and the mentally insane.

One mentally ill inmate known as Jerry committed suicide in 1920 by slitting his own throat. Another inmate stabbed himself to death while on the lawn. Another convict named Lizzie died in jail while she was waiting to be transported to the mental hospital. All of these inmates are thought to be "resident spirits" here today.

Not only did executions, assassinations, and suicides take place here, but so did child births. Female inmates or jailer's family members who were pregnant gave birth here at the jail. In those days it was often a long drive to the nearest hospital. You had the babies pretty much wherever you were when the time came.

The Haunted Jail

The first official paranormal investigation that was done here was in 2009 by C.A.P.E. Paranormal Investigations. They reported abundant activity from hearing cell doors opening and closing to hearing voices and footsteps. Some of their investigators even reported being touched by a ghostly presence. There is so much activity in the building that Northeast Florida's local paranormal television show, *Local Haunts*, filmed their pilot episode here. Since then several paranormal groups have come here to investigate for themselves.

Historic Haunts Investigations came here in March 2013 and the building didn't let us down. We had many of the same experiences as C.A.P.E. and the Local Haunts teams had. Vishi Garig who is a docent with The Clay County Archives and a member of C.A.P.E. Paranormal Investigations announced to the spirit inmates that it was visitation day. That seemed to draw them all out.

Historic Haunts Investigates Too

We started our investigation on the second floor. We introduced ourselves to the spirits after setting up our equipment. Within just a few moments, the activity began.

We had a flash light set up as you enter the upstairs cell block to the right, along with a K2 EMF meter which picks up on fluctuations in the electromagnetic field (EMF). Spirits are believed to manipulate this when manifesting or affecting the material world. We also had a real time RTEVP Recorder recording in hopes of picking up any EVP's (Electronic Voice Phenomenon). In addition, we had a full

Interior shot, row of cells at the Old Clay County Jail

11

spectrum camera set up looking down the cell block to capture movement or anything coming in or out of the cells. When I asked, "We hear its visiting day. Would anyone like to visit with us?" The K2 Meter spiked up to the red light, the flash light turned on, and the full spectrum camera turned off. It was a brand new battery so this shouldn't have happened. Eager to capture video we tried to replace the battery and restart. When that failed we even tried to run it off the power cord, the camera refused to work! When we finished the investigation that night, I tested it as soon as I got home. It worked perfectly! Apparently the spirits didn't want to be on video that evening.

With all the trouble the camera was giving us my tech advisor asked the spirits if they didn't want to be captured on film; both the flash light and the K2 meter lit up! We decided to bag the camera and try some of the other equipment. I put a Mel Meter K2 Hybrid out to see if we could get any activity on that. This meter, being a hybrid, gives you a digital reading on the EMF and the temperature. The Mel K2 feature, besides being digital, lights up in case you are far away and cannot see the digital reading. We pulled this other equipment out and again attempted to interact with the jail's paranormal populace.

We asked the inmates if they would like us to try and get them some poker cards, we received no response. We asked about coffee, again no response. So we asked about cigarettes and candy, and with that inquiry got a response on all the equipment. Eventually the activity decreased.

We decided to go over to the left side of the second floor to check out the cell block over there. Once situated with equipment in place, we decided to try something unusual. Deric asked if anyone there new this song and he began to whistle the first part of Camptown Races. To our surprise, instead of silence or hearing a whistle back we heard a verbal, "Do-Da Do-Da." We had similar success with the old "Shave and a Hair Cut" bit with Deric announcing and knocking out the first part and the jail's spirits knocking to complete the "two bits".

As we continued questioning the spirits there was a perceptible change in the atmosphere of the area. I felt as though there was another female present other than me. Could it be Lizzie, said to haunt this area? I asked, "Lizzie, is that you?" The flash light turned itself on. Suddenly I had a strong feeling of fear and asked her if there was a jailer she was afraid of and if he was approaching. The flash light and the K2 meter both became very active. I got the distinct feeling that Lizzie's spirit had temporarily flown the coup. After that, it got very quiet on that side of the jail. We decided to move downstairs.

As we descended the staircase to investigate the downstairs we started hearing all kinds of noise from where we had just been upstairs. We heard a cell door slam shut and footsteps walking around. Were they glad we left or were they trying to figure out where we were going next?

We were sitting in the middle of the hallway at the very end of the first floor where I felt drawn to put a flash light by each door way at the end. One flash light was to my right and the other one was to my left with the Mel Meter in the middle of the hall. As we started to do an EVP session one of us asked, "Are there any children here?" The flash light on the right lit up and the Mel Meter showed a significant temperature drop of five degrees. We continued to ask questions and were able to determine (based on positive light and meter readings) that the spirit affecting the equipment was a little boy who 5 years old was. As we continued to talk to him, the other light started frantically going on and off. Deric then asked, "Is there someone else here?" The flashlight on the left lit up so bright we started doing a question and answer session with it too. The other spirit was a boy as well and was 12 years old. They didn't seem to know each other, but they both knew Sheriff Cherry. Funny how we mentioned several of the former Sheriffs and the only one we got a response to was Cherry. We continued to talk to the boys and we did discover that both of them loved it when the train came by. The jail is located just across the street from the train tracks. Funny thing, while we were doing the EVP session we heard the train whistle and we continued to try and talk with the boys and the flash lights stopped. After the train was gone, we asked if they left to go watch the train and both the lights lit up again.

The hour was getting late and we decided to call the investigation for the night. We packed up all our gear. Before departing we shared with Vishi some of the experiences we'd had. After hearing them and just as we were about to go she turned back toward the building and said, "It's time for lockdown. There will be a head count in the morning." She said this seems to keep the spirits from following anyone home.

The Old Clay County Jail is certifiably haunted in our book and they are open to investigations at a very reasonable price. The money is put back into the archives to keep the building preserved and all the artifacts inside. The setting is ideal too. Where else can you investigate creepy cells full of cobwebs, peeling paint and rusting bunks? It's a great place to train your group or even for an experienced investigator to connect with the paranormal.

If you are interested in investigating the old jail please contact Vishi Garig at 904-371-0027 or go online for all the details at archives.clayclerk.com

*Historic photo of the Gallows at
Old Clay County Jail
Courtesy of Clay County Archives*

THE GHOSTLY STEAMER

St. Johns River (Mandarin Point), Jacksonville, Florida

A scale replica of the Maple Leaf on display at Jacksonville's Museum of Science & History

A river runs through it, Northeast Florida that is. In this case, the river is the St. John's, a 310 mile long body of water and one of the few rivers within the U.S. that runs north. Further, while it feeds or flows into numerous other lakes and rivers, it also winds through or borders twelve counties, including three of the state's largest. With all of these areas near the St. Johns, it's no wonder that it served as the main route of transportation for centuries for the Native Americans, French, Spanish, and English colonists, as well as many others.

As northeast Florida developed, the St. John's River became the "interstate highway" of the time, causing steamboat and other traffic to thrive. Riverboats were popular in their time, revolutionizing travel and causing many to move close to the rivers for easy access to transportation. Harriett Beacher Stowe and her husband built their winter home in 1867 in Mandarin on the St. John's River because of this. While there are many stories of those along the St. Johns and on the river itself from this time; there's one boat in particular we'll move "full steam ahead" to discuss.

A Canadian Import

On June 18, 1851, the Great Lakes passenger steamship Maple Leaf set to sea from its construction site in Kingston, Ontario for the Donald Bethune Company. She was a beautiful ship, 181 feet long, 25 feet wide at the beam, and displacing 398 tons. Running the entire length of the main deck was a passenger deck that held a pilot house, passenger staterooms, a 130 foot long "saloon", main dining area, and officer's quarters. Above the saloon deck, the ship's lifeboats were stored on the "hurricane deck". She was a grand lady of great lakes ferrying passengers and freight between Canadian and American ports. When the Bethune Company started to flounder, she was sold to a company based in Rochester, New York in April 1855.

It was during her tenure in Rochester that she would enjoy the high point of her celebrity status. Newspapers reported her departures and arrivals daily on Lake Ontario, and passengers reported grand excursions with bands and great opportunities to dance. She even housed excursions to meet the Prince of Wales and his entourage in 1860, and to see the celebrated "Blondin" (tightrope walker and acrobat) perform on the high wire above Niagara Falls. Unfortunately, her glory days on the Lake were numbered, as railroad competition and the outbreak of the Civil War put an end to her river excursions. In August of 1862, the Maple Leaf was sold to a Boston firm, who then chartered her into service for the United States.

A Riverboat Goes to War

The Maple Leaf steamed her way to Boston, where she would be overhauled and converted for use as a military transport. On September 8th, she arrived at Fort Monroe, a union stronghold, for her new tour of duty. During her early days in the service, the Maple Leaf routinely ferried supplies, equipment and Union troops along the Atlantic Coast. On June 9, 1863 she was hijacked by a group of Confederate prisoners she was delivering to Fort Delaware. It was two months after the hijacking (and perhaps because of the embarrassing incident) that the Maple Leaf was given new duties.

The New York Volunteer Infantry and the Steamship

The Maple Leaf was assigned a supportive roll for Major General Quincy Gilmore's siege of Charleston. Among other things she would be ferrying members of the 112th New York Volunteer Infantry. On one occasion the 112th were brigaded with the 169th New York Volunteers for a series of skirmishes and missions. During this time it was believed the men repeatedly helped themselves to items from as many as 17 abandoned plantation homes, returning to camp with their treasures.

In February of 1864, after the Union suffered a loss at the Battle of Olustee, the Maple Leaf and the 112th were assigned a support role to General Seymour's Florida expedition (including the rest of the Brigade - the 169th New York Volunteers and the 13th Indiana Volunteers). The steamship transported the men to Jacksonville then returned to their prior camp for their supplies and personal belongings. With only the St. John's separating the two warring factions in many places, she made her way down the river on the evening of March 31st. She stopped in Palatka and dropped off a detachment of Massachusetts cavalry and equipment, but she didn't go unnoticed.

The Sinking of the Maple Leaf

Historical marker on Jacksonville's Riverwalk

As the Maple Leaf passed, she and her passengers were being watched from the west bank of the St. Johns. In anticipation of her return trip, Captain E. Pliny Bryan and five other Confederate soldiers placed a dozen "torpedoes" (what we would today call a mine) along the path the Maple Leaf had just taken. At 4 a.m. the morning of April 1st, as the pilot was returning from Palatka and neared Mandarin Point on the St. Johns, the ship struck one of the Confederate torpedoes. A tremendous explosion occurred about 30 feet from ship's bow, killing four crewmen. The night sky was filled with black smoke and fire as the crew tried to escape. In less than two minutes water rushed in and almost all of the Maple Leaf was submerged. Only part of the smoke stacks and the top of the wheelhouse remained above water.

The lifeboats were put to use as 58 passengers and crew left the wreck (4 Confederate prisoners were reportedly refused places on the lifeboats). A few hours later, a Union Navy Gunboat surveyed the carnage and deemed the boat and her cargo a total loss. At the time of her sinking the Maple Leaf was laden with the supplies and baggage of three Union regiments (including items they pilfered from plantations) and two sutlers stores (about $20,000 value). What remained above the water line was burned when Bryan and his confederates returned the next day. The Maple Leaf remained a navigation hazard in the river until enough of her upper area was removed after the war for safe boat passage. After that she and her location were all but forgotten, buried under layers of mud and silt.

The Maple Leaf Rediscovered

In 1981, intense historical research determined the approximate location in the river where the Maple Leaf wreck lay submerged in the brackish and muddy St. Johns. In 1985, electronic equipment produced the first site survey; the first excavations on site were done by divers in 1988. Since then, over 3,000 individual artifacts have been recovered. Many of these items are on display for the public at the Jacksonville Museum of Science and History. In 1994, the site was designated a National Historic Landmark. Historic markers on shore in downtown Jacksonville (15 miles from the site) and the suburb of Orange Park describe the incident and the story of the Maple Leaf's demise. The Maple Leaf is considered by many to be the largest single repository of Civil War artifacts in the world.

Historical marker in Clay County (the opposite side of the river) on River Street

The Paranormal Paddleboat

There have been many reports around the Mandarin Point area on the St. Johns River describing a ghostly steam boat seen late at night floating along the river. Some people have even reported that on the anniversary date of her sinking you can see smoke and hear the screams of the men trying to get to safety coming from the river. One gentleman told me that he saw a transparent steamboat floating along the eastern shore of the river then all of a sudden it vanished. There have been many other reports by boaters and those on shore with details and descriptions that match. Apparently the Maple Leaf still steams down the St. Johns, but now it seems her smokestacks emit the ethereal energies of an Historic Haunt!

SAND, SURF & SPIRITS AT THE CASA MARINA HOTEL

Casa Marina Hotel, Jacksonville Beach, Florida

Who doesn't like a day at the beach? In the mid-1920's Jacksonville Beach was touted as the 'World's Finest Beach'. Everyone who was anyone found themselves traveling south to Florida and its hot spots. Amidst its brightly lit boardwalk, colorful casinos and amazing amusement rides was a radiant and refined hotel that would witness the splendor of the era and the history making times that followed, the Casa Marina.

Jacksonville Beach's Casa Marina

The Glamorous Hotel and Her Past

The Casa Marina Hotel is a beautiful building ideally positioned on Jacksonville Beach. The grand opening was June 6th, 1925 and two hundred guests celebrated it at the hotel salon. This Spanish Mediterranean style hotel brought a first to Jacksonville Beach. It was a fire proof building with an automatic sprinkler system. The two story building originally had sixty guest rooms in its two story structure.

During its glory days, the hotel was rumored to host a who's who of politicians, prohibition-era gangsters, and Hollywood stars. Note worthies like The Duke and Duchess of Windsor, Al Capone, John D. Rockefeller, Harry Truman, and F.D.R. were believed to have stayed here as well as Hollywood greats like Charlie Chaplin, Buster Keaton, Fatty Arbuckle, Laurel and Hardy, and Katharine Hepburn.

During WWII the US Government appropriated the hotel as military housing. After the war it went back to being privately owned and changed hands several times. At one point it housed a vintage clothing store, a tea room, and even the Casa Marina Apartments, with thirty-seven apartments and a restaurant. During this time a third-story penthouse was added and it drew some attention with its view of the beach. In addition, for some time, on the south side of the building was a large swimming pool. Locals have shared stories about how on hot summer days they would do cannon balls out the second floor window into the pool. Today there is nothing more here than an empty lot between the building and the parking area.

The building is now known as the Casa Marina Hotel and Restaurant with twenty-three bedrooms with parlor suites. There is also The Penthouse Lounge with an amazing view of the Atlantic Ocean. This historic beauty not only has a rich past, but a haunted one as well. There are actually several spirits still believed to be lingering here.

The Casa Marina's Ghostly Guests

The first ghost I want to mention is found in room #209. The room is located on the second floor in the center portion of the building. The back story attached to this room involves a day some years ago when a house keeper was reportedly tidying up. She went about her job cleaning the window. While cleaning it she failed to realize there was a large hairline crack in the glass. Suddenly the glass in the window broke into multiple shards and one of the long sharp pieces impaled her. She died in the room.

While investigating the room, the entire Historic Haunts Investigations team felt a presence. This presence, while not a negative one, was still strong nonetheless. It felt as if there was a female spirit present. She seemed very lonely and was seeking company. When we finished our investigation of the room it was almost as if she didn't want us to leave. The bedroom area where we gathered while investigating (and near the windows) was much colder than the parlor of the room, a fact confirmed by our meters which detected a good ten degrees temperature difference. Noting this change and the fact that this would be a rather large cold spot; we thoroughly explored the room and found no drafts, and that neither the air conditioning nor the heat had been on during our session.

We gathered our equipment and moved to room #215, another spot believed to be very active. This was actually the room I slept in. Earlier in the day I had felt something before the investigation even began when I went up to drop off my bags and equipment. There was such a peaceful presence in the room. We were investigating 5 rooms total that night, and had the choice to sleep in whichever room we wanted. When I entered #215 something told me it was my room and it was almost as though arms were wrapped around me inviting me in. It was definitely a female presence, and she felt very motherly and nurturing.

During the actual investigation we set the equipment up in this room, but didn't get any unusual readings at all, however, I did pick up on the female presence which was there. Later I had a very restful night's sleep once the investigation was over (a rarity since I usually find myself wired and replaying everything through my head afterwards). We didn't uncover any detailed back story on the room, just a roll call of weird occurrences which were repeatedly reported by guests and staff.

We moved on to the investigation of room #101, which we found very interesting. We had cameras, meters, and flashlights set up all around the bedroom area and the parlor and prepared to do an EVP (electronic voice phenomenon) session in the parlor. I felt once again as if there was some kind of presence in the room. We began asking several questions and received no responses or readings on the

19

meters, when all of the sudden there was an extremely bright flash from the camera viewer at the back of the full spectrum camera. We were all surprised by the incident because we'd never experienced a flash of this type coming from the back of the camera. The flash was so bright that an entire portion of the room lit up. We all turned our attention towards the camera. It was still working just fine but I wanted to review it immediately. I rewound the video to the point of the flash; the picture was so bright it was almost white. You could hear the three of us comment on it. Then I noticed the video had captured a dark shadow darting in front of the camera (immediately following the flash and the comments).

Afterwards the whole atmosphere of the room changed. It was as if the energy in the room had drained and quickly left. Our instruments picked up nothing further in the room.

We continued on to room #216. This was one of the few areas that had something of an explanation for the paranormal activity. The story behind this room was that in the 1930's or 1940's a man had committed suicide. After setting up all the equipment in the room, we proceeded, determined to get some answers about what really happened with the spirit believed to still be residing here.

Between EVP's and responses with the flash light we found out the entity had died in the 1940's and according to the Q&A we executed he didn't commit suicide. His death was apparently due to a business deal gone wrong and the loss of a great deal of money, not only his, but his partner's money as well. The spirit was directing us to believe his partner shot him and made it look like a suicide.

While we were getting good evidence on our equipment, I was getting strong feelings of my own. The spirit in this room was not an evil one. He just wanted people that have heard the story of his "suicide" to know the truth. I also got the feeling he was curious about the people coming and going in the room. During the question and answer session with the flash light test (which is actually a very easy and inexpensive ghost hunting tool**), I was sitting on the floor asking my questions, when something suddenly grabbed my ankle. It wasn't painful or malicious in any way just playful. We asked him if he wanted us to go and he replied no. We asked if he enjoyed having company and he replied yes. Despite the successful interaction we were experiencing, the investigation had been going on for some time. Our visiting spirit seemed to be growing weaker in the lighting of his responses. We decided we were going to take a short break. We asked if he would like us to stay and return, he replied yes with a positive response causing the flashlight to get brighter than it had previously. After a short break we returned as promised. As soon as we opened the door to reenter after the break, the light started flickering on and off as though he was excited to see us.

We asked more questions and received responses on unimportant matters before I noticed the replies once again growing weaker. I had just begun to try and learn the identity of the man's partner and suspected killer. When suddenly I felt as if our friend was gone and a new unfriendly spirit had entered the room. I felt intense pressure on my lungs as if they were collapsing and it became very hard to breathe. I had to leave the room to catch my breath and I felt as if I might get sick. Another team member asked (as I relayed my suspicions of the new presence and left the room) if it was the entity pushing my chest and it replied yes. Some of my team came to check on me. We weren't getting any more readings in the room when I returned and defiantly replied, "We know what you did!" I felt this darker presence retreat and all energy in the room seemed to return to normal. Getting no other readings or responses we gathered our stuff and moved on.

The last area we focused on was the north wing hallway and the children's spirits believed to be there. A playful duo reportedly loves running up and down the hall at all hours of the evening. People have actually called the front desk complaining on the children in the hallway when there wasn't a child in the entire hotel. People have heard the giggles literally right outside their room doors, and when they open the door, there's nothing to be seen. We investigated the claims associated with the area thoroughly, but got no response.

The Hotel's Other Ghost Stories

Those were the main îhauntedî rooms described to us in our research, but the hotel boasts other suspected haunts. A shadowy figure has been observed on the southern staircase. In addition, an unseen presence has reportedly been encountered that enjoys tripping people as they walk up the main staircase (typically near the 7th step). We looked into these areas as well, but discovered no evidence.

The Casa Marina is a beautiful historic gem and a great venue for weddings or for a quiet couple's getaway. The spirits in the hotel are generally friendly though mischievous. The spirits in the Penthouse Lounge are tasty too (and what a view). Whether you're looking for a ghostly retreat or a beachside getaway, Historic Haunts highly recommends this grand old lady.

**Author's Note:
The flash light test is very simple. You take a Maglite Flashlight and twist the end so that it almost turns on. You shake it to make sure it doesn't relight without some effort to turn it. Then you set it down in a place where it will not roll and you explain to the spirit the flash light, lantern, candle or torch (terminology depending on what century the ghost is from) will not harm them. When you ask a question tell them to tap or touch the light for yes. If they are willing they will make contact with the flashlight and the light will come on. If their answer is no then ask them not to touch it. Alternately you can also have more than one flashlight, one for yes, one for no, etc. There are other variations too, although for clarity's sake I recommend spacing out the flashlights. The spirits can't always tell the difference between colored flashlights.**

THE MERMAID'S GHOST

33 Star / Ginger's Place, Jacksonville Beach, Florida

(These two companion pieces ran back to back in the Florida Times Union, they were edited for space and content. I write a bi-monthly column for the newspaper under the caption "Ghostly Shores". They appear here with permission from the newspaper and with additional content)

Photo courtesy of 33 star

33 Star

You don't have to be a rock star to enter 33 Star at Jacksonville Beach, but it sure makes you feel like one. The building that is now 33 Star was built in the 1950's as Ossi's Supermarket. When Thressa Anderson bought the building in 2011, she turned it into an amazing Rock-N-Roll boutique and concert venue.

While remodeling for the store the building went through some major renovations. Just like debris from the building, renovations can sometimes also stir up the paranormal world. Funny thing is, the ghost who visits here on a frequent basis is not some long gone rocker or ghostly groupie, but is actually from next door. In fact, right next door to 33 Star is Ginger's Place, a favorite Jacksonville Beach drinking establishment. While Ginger's ghost is experienced at both locations, her history and the bar that bears her name is a ghostly tale for another day. Still, one thing you must know about Ginger is that when she lived, she was all about sparkle and glitz. With all the rhinestones, bejeweled chandeliers, and even the glamorous stage found at 33 Star, it's easy to see why Ginger might make frequent personal appearances.

For Thressa and her crew, the activity began when they were in the middle of the remodel. They started finding dimes throughout the store in the strangest places. They would completely clean and sweep an area and turn around to find a dime. Customers have even had a dime appear out of nowhere, right in front of them. The staff insists that with only a brief interruption, the sudden appearance of the dimes has continued with customers and workers even to this day. "The place often has that, you're not alone feeling," says Eddy Kalanoc, 33 Star's Operations Manager. Eddy has also experienced the dimes appearing out of nowhere and shared, "We kept finding these dimes so I decided to Google it and see what it meant." Eddy's research coincided with many of my past experiences, dimes and small change are a way for many spirits to say hello. I have experienced this with pennies in the past. On this Thressa remarked, "It would be nice if dollars would appear instead."

Keith O'Rourke, 33 Star's Internet Sales Manager, elaborated further, "I went into the convenience store to get a drink, pulled out my wallet, and there was a dime inside my wallet. This is the kind of strange stuff that happens around here." It was a funny coincidence, that while Keith was sharing his story with me, the light directly above his head (a brand new 7 year LED light bulb) got really bright, then went completely out! Keith confirmed that apparently, Ginger messes with the lights too.

In addition to the lights, the staff has also reported the dressing room doors opening and slamming shut on their own. One customer got spooked when she was patted on the back while trying on clothes. Most of the paranormal experiences described by customers and staff seem to be centered on drawing attention. Sometimes this happens even when there's no one there to get attention from. One morning when the staff came in, there was a shelf lying on the floor and shirts were everywhere. The store has security cameras throughout with night vision ability and Thressa and the others decided to replay the previous night's video to see what happened. Thressa, Keith, and Eddy all shared the same story about what the video showed them. "There was a ball of light floating around in front of the shelf sporadically with no definite direction. Then all of a sudden, wham! It slammed into the shelf, the shelf collapsed and shirts went everywhere!"

The disruptive behavior and mysterious dimes continued until one evening in mid to late 2012. On this night while closing, Thressa and a female employee heard a disembodied voice saying very disrespectful things. Thressa was furious and shouted out to the empty room, "If you are going to disrespect us, you can just leave!!" The girl closing with her was worried about making the spirit mad, but Thressa, undaunted, stood up to the disrespectful spirit and said, "It's my place, not hers." The activity stopped after that until December 2012 when Jessica Crawford, 33 Star's Formal Specialist, had an experience. She had just learned that her father had passed away and she went into the back upset about the news. She looked down and discovered two dimes. She felt this was Ginger's way of trying to comfort her. Jessica mentioned this to her boss Thressa. Thressa told Ginger, or whoever it was, that they could come back as long as they showed them respect, and once again, the dimes began to reappear.

The activity at 33 Star even drew the attention of a Jacksonville based Paranormal themed TV show. They investigated here and actually saw a full body apparition walking through the wall as if it were leaving and heading next door to Ginger's Place. Maybe it was Ginger stopping by for her daily visit, or maybe she was checking on some great vintage concert gear? Like the staff at 33 Star, and the TV show team, I too had an interesting experience while researching this story. After doing the interviews for this article I had to run a few errands. Like many of us I ran my errands with debit cards and credit cards, I had no cash on me at all. When I got home, I discovered several dimes in my pocket that weren't there before! Coincidence? Only Ginger knows for sure.

Cocktails and Strange Tales at Ginger's Place

Have you ever seen a mermaid? If you've visited "Ginger's Place" on Third Street South in Jacksonville Beach you might have. In this case the mermaid would be Darlene Edith Payson, known as "Ginger" Payson to many who knew her. Pictures of Ginger in her prime adorn the walls of this popular beaches

Ginger's Place & the Silhouettes

bar. During her younger days, before opening the bar, she was also known as Ginger Lani or as Tiza, The Girl in the Goldfish Bowl. Ginger not only did mermaid and underwater shows in a portable tank, but was also a star of vaudeville burlesque shows. She traveled up and down the Atlantic coast performing and gaining notoriety for her unique talents. When she retired, she and her husband, Ziggy, bought the building now known as Ginger's Place.

Like its owner, Ginger's Place had an interesting past prior to her purchase of it in 1976 and the opening of the current bar. It reportedly was built sometime around 1950 and over the years has housed several different businesses. Many of these businesses came and went as quickly as Ginger's traveling shows. Among them a fast-food store, a glass bar, a grocery store, and a dress shop. Oddly enough, the provocative silhouettes of the dress shop mannequins helped draw interest to this casual beaches bar when they were thought to be "looking" from the upstairs windows. One other successful business of note occupied the space during the 1960's, and was popular with residents of Jacksonville Beach, Ossi's Grocery Store. Ossi's eventually sought easier access and parking and had a new building built just next door. This building would eventually become another Jacksonville Beach fixture, 33 Star (featured in the last Ghostly Shores column). Still, despite the areas many incarnations, my research unearthed only sparse tales of paranormal activity in Ginger's Place until after her death from a stroke in 2003, at age 79.

Needless to say, one of the spirits believed to be active at Ginger's Place is of course, Ginger. Ironically, she never believed in ghosts and actually had friendly arguments with her granddaughter, Amanda Sams, about the topic.

After talking to members of the family and staff, and researching stories from visitors and bar patrons alike, it's very clear that whether she believed it in life or not, Ginger's spirit is present! She seems to not only make paranormal appearances to her public at the show biz themed 33 Star next door, but even more frequently at the bar that bears her name!

If you missed the last article in my Ghostly Shores column about 33 Star, it detailed reports about Ginger's ghost and the appearance of dimes throughout their store. The sudden and unexplained appearance of dimes and spare change in general is thought by many in the paranormal field to be a means of communication, a way for many spirits to say hello. Like 33 Star next door, dimes often appear at Ginger's Place typically under many of the same inexplicable circumstances. However, after talking to Ginger's family I learned they may have discovered an even more pleasant reason for the ghostly spare change. One of Ginger's granddaughters and a manager and bartender at Ginger's, Amanda Sams, (who finds the dimes at work and home) shared a story with me. She told me that when they were doing renovations they found an old price sign from the bar when drinks were 10 cents each. Amanda said "I wonder if maybe Ginger is buying drinks for people she likes? She did used to do that when she was alive."

Ginger seems to have other means besides dimes to make her presence known. Samantha Robenolt, another one of Ginger's granddaughters and a fellow manager/bartender at the bar, has experienced some of the same things as her sister Amanda. Samantha said her grandmother would often times tap her on the leg to get her attention. She did this to her family and friends and Samantha and Amanda have both experienced this sensation at the bar multiple times with no visible source.

Samantha and Amanda elaborated giving other reasons they sometimes know their grandmother's spirit is present at Ginger's Place. There is a calendar on the wall with an adjustable area to enter "today's date" and the year so the bartenders know drinkers are of age when checking i.d. The calendar has a tendency to change the date on its own. Not to a

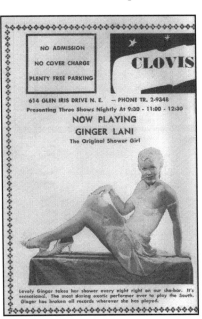

Ginger in her heyday
courtesy of Ginger's Place

random date, but to September 27th, Ginger's birthday. Further, a Miller Lite sign on the back of the register has been seen flipping up in the air and over the tip jar in front of the register by both of them. One of their new employees actually witnessed it as well, and then had a strange feeling of a hand being run through his hair. Sam exclaimed, "He doesn't even have hair!" Strange occurrences like this go on all the time here at Ginger's.

It isn't just Ginger's family that frequently encounters her ghost here. I also spoke with bartender Michael and he shared an interesting experience with a new patron to the bar. "This woman I had never seen before came in to the bar and ordered a drink. I poured it for her and she asked about the woman behind the bar in the doorway that was staring at me? I turned around and saw a woman, who I knew, was Ginger. She floated from the doorway to the back and vanished. I turned back around to the woman at the bar, the money for her tab was on the counter and she was leaving. She was as white as a ghost!" Besides Michael, Samantha and Amanda, many others have claimed to see a female apparition the same height and size as Ginger sometimes floating on air or walking through doors. Other times they catch a glimpse of her out of the corner of their eye and when they go to investigate, she's gone.

While working on this story, Samantha sent me a message that a friend of hers had recently gone to the cigarette machine in the bar and bought a pack of cigarettes. If you put only bills in the machine it gives fifty cents change. In this particular case, Samantha's friend didn't get her two quarters change and never heard the change drop so she checked the machine anyway. She found three dimes, a pretty neat trick since Samantha told me this particular machine isn't capable of giving dimes as change. Was someone playing a trick or was Ginger making her presence known again?

Whether tapping legs, flipping signs or dispensing dimes, Ginger's ghost and stories of other spirits at Ginger's Place have drawn interest from many including some ghostly research groups. Fortunately, there is nothing malicious about the reports of Ginger or the other alleged spirits here. A medium visited the bar and claims that there are 13 different spirits residing here. Whether this is true or not, I don't know, but I do know a bar can certainly serve up some spirits. Perhaps Ginger's activities have drawn a few of her paranormal friends to this beaches area haunt. I guess I will find out when my team, Historic Haunts Investigations, investigates the building. After so generously sharing their stories, Ginger's granddaughters have graciously allowed us to set up an investigation. I am anxious to see what our investigation turns up and find out more about Ginger and some of the other spirits. Maybe I should empty my change purse first?

ANCIENT CITY'S LITTLE LOVE NEST
Ancient City Inn, St. Augustine, Florida

St. Augustine is no stranger to ghosts. In fact, it is considered one of the most haunted cities in America. Many of the local ghost stories center on tragic events or deaths. There are a few, however, who seem to have pleasant stories and pleasant haunts. One of these is the Ancient City Inn of St. Augustine.

Ancient City Inn

The Inn's Colorful Past

We can't continue without telling a little bit of the history of the inn. Charles Sequi (a Minorcan, whose family had been in town since the 1700's) was a good man with a fondness for raising and training carrier pigeons. Charles owned a book store on St. George Street which serviced guest of Henry Flaglerís two St. Augustine hotels. He also had carrier pigeons. He sold his original lot of trained birds to a wealthy publisher from New York (a friend of Flagler's). He used the money from the sale to purchase a tract of land north of town and build a Victorian style home. He and his wife, Maude, completed the house in 1910 and lived here with their daughter Martha Lee.

After the house was built Charles resumed his love of bird keeping. Behind the house he kept the pigeons he trained and used to carry messages (especially to Cuba), as well as horses, and his carriage. Every day like clockwork, around 2 p.m. Charles would leave his book store, rush home, run upstairs and change from his business clothes into work clothes. He would then go outside and feed the pigeons and horses. Afterwards he would then come inside, eat lunch, change back into his business suit, and head back to work.

Charles continued his punctual lunches until his death. After he passed he left his home to his widowed wife Maude and daughter Martha Lee. The house remained a private residence until Martha Lee was in her 20's; after that her mother took in boarders to try and make ends meet.

It was during this time that they took in a boarder who was apparently a handsome colonel. It didnít take long for Martha Lee to fall in love with the colonel and he in love with her. His boarding room was on the second floor and right next door to Martha Lee's. Their love affair blossomed until one day when Maude came up to Martha Lee's room and found her daughter and the colonel in a compromising position. Maude was enraged and kicked him out of the house, forbidding him to ever return. He moved to California and Martha Lee never saw him again.

She was heartbroken. Martha Lee never moved on, she spent the rest of the time at her home alone, the only man in her life being her cat Toby. She grieved for the colonel until her death. She died a spinster at the age of 89.

Before she passed Martha Lee sold her home in 1989, and it has been an inn ever since. Carri and Will Donnan bought the inn in 2000. They have operated and lived in the inn for over 10 years. They both consider themselves sensitives and are very familiar with the happy haunts still residing here.

Will & Carri's Experiences and the Happy Haunts Within

When the Donnans first bought the Inn, one of the rooms upstairs was a dark green color and it felt heavy and sad. It was a depressing room. It reminded them of the military so they nicknamed it the Colonel's Room.

Sometime later, after talking with neighbors they found out that the room had actually been the colonelís when he lived there. One day Carri was tired of that deep, dark, depressing green and decided to paint it a very girlie pink. Immediately the room lost its sadness and felt much more happy and uplifting.

While Will and Carri were settling in, getting a feel for the place and all the creaks the house made; they had their first paranormal experience. One day while Carri was downstairs the front door flew open and a shadowy figure floated quickly through the room and stomped up the stairs. Then a door upstairs slammed shut. Startled, Carri looked around amazed by what she just experienced. Will had heard the noise and came running from his work shop in the back of the house to see what caused it. They both noticed it was about 2 p.m. on the clock. To this day like clockwork, the Donnans experience this phenomenon on a daily basis. Apparently Charles is still rushing home from the bookstore to have lunch and feed the animals at the Inn.

Another happy haunt the Donnans and guests have encountered here at the inn is Martha Lee. Her room is the most active and we experienced just that. Initially, we didnít know any of the exact details of the haunted room except that it was Martha Leeís. We found out, after the fact, that everything we experienced had been experienced by many others.

Our Investigation

Historic Haunts Investigations investigated the beautiful Ancient City Inn in November 2012 and the spirits who reside there didnít disappoint us. Our experiences began during the set up. When we first get to a location (like many paranormal investigators) we do a base reading on everything and set all the equipment up. During the setup, my husband Deric -who is also the tech adviser for Historic Haunts Investigations-left the room to grab a few more things before we started the investigation. I was in Martha Lee's room alone. As I continued gathering base readings I heard the clip clop, clip clop, clip clop of a horse out on the street. I thought to myself, "how cool, one of the carriages is going by," so I grabbed my still camera and went outside to take a photo of it. As I left the room and continued down the back stairs I was still hearing the clip clop noises. I got outside and looked towards the street, but there was nothing there. I was still hearing the sounds. So I went around to the back of the house thinking it was coming from the back street. As I headed towards the street, still hearing the sound, I found nothing. There wasn't a carriage or horse anywhere in the vicinity of the Inn! I shared this story with Carri the next day and apparently she too had experienced this.

Deric returned and I relayed the experience to him while we finished setting up and preparing for the investigation. We tried out the equipment, and once satisfied began asking many different questions hoping to capture some good evidence. Unfortunately, while we continued to studiously perform the tasks we do on every investigation we really weren't getting anywhere.

Then Deric started acting a little abnormal for an investigation. He is often fun loving, but generally very meticulous when on an investigation. In this case he started getting very amorous and frisky. I replied. "Seriously, we are trying to investigate." Slightly defeated he tried to focus back on investigating. We gave it a little longer, but no spirits seemed to want to communicate. So we decided to let the cameras and digital recorders run and turn in. Deric was still feeling very frisky and I told him to stop, we were after all, still trying to get ghostly evidence on camera, plus we had to get up very early the next morning. The next day upon researching what other guests have experienced in Martha Lee's room, we discovered she has a way of "kindling flames" and helping couples get together. Some guests have even described being love drunk with a feeling like they were under the influence of an aphrodisiac. I hope Martha Lee wasn't upset with me for not being in the mood.

As we blissfully nodded off into a silent slumber in our comfortable bed, the paranormal activity began. During the night I felt a hand on my face slowly pulling the hair back off my face and caressing my cheek. I woke up thinking it was Deric, but he was sound asleep. I also noticed upon waking that the blanket was pulled up over my shoulders. I was tucked in and that is not how I went to bed or how I usually sleep. This is apparently another one of Martha Lee's ways of letting people know she is around.

A couple of hours later I woke up yet again as I felt something jump on the bed around my feet. Still half asleep I briefly thought I was at home in bed and our cat Griffin had jumped on the bed. I suddenly realized we weren't home and there was nothing on the bed where I felt the weight on my feet. It felt like two little paws kneading my feet and the blanket. I realized it was probably the ghost of Martha Lee's favorite pet Toby, rumored to still be lingering here at the Inn. I said, "Ok kitty, lie down and go to sleep." Many other people have experienced the ghost cat Toby at the Ancient City Inn.

The next morning, when we got up and started loading up the equipment, we discovered the cameras had shut down in the middle of the night and we later found out there was nothing on the digital recorders. I told Deric what I had experienced in the night. He then shared with me what happened to him. He said he woke up in the middle of the night and the bathroom light was on (despite the fact that he had turned it off before crashing for the night). While he laid there perplexed something passed in front of the bathroom door and blocked out most of the light. He said it appeared to be the size and shape of a large man. Maybe it was the general wanting to know why we were in Martha Lee's room. We wouldn't be the first to encounter him; other guests have reported seeing him as well.

At the end of our investigation what we did realize is that The Ancient City Inn is a magnificent place to stay in the nationís oldest city. Carri and Will have a contagious and wonderful energy that will pick you up the moment you meet them. Besides being innkeepers, Rev. Carri Donnan is a spiritualist psychic/medium who trained in Lilydale New York and her husband Will is a Shaman and a medium. They do readings during the day, aura photography, and other fascinating things such as past life regressions.

This is also a great place to stay to rekindle the romance in your relationship, meet a ghost, or contact a deceased loved one. It is truly a peaceful and welcoming retreat from the hustle and bustle of busy life and a welcoming Historic Haunt.

Author's Note:
If you decide to spend the night at the Ancient City Inn and are looking for more paranormal happenings, make sure you check out the **2 Ghouls**. *2 Ghouls offers a fresh spin on ghost tours. They take you on an escapade through St. Augustine's decadent Victorian Era of excess and spiritualism (and brightly colored homes like the Ancient City Inn's "painted lady"). Small groups in intimate settings allow for a personalized experience. They are also available for private events and investigations of the Old Jail. Contact the 2 Ghouls, Tina and Brandy at www.2ghouls.com for more information on investigations at the Old Jail, The Toasted Ghost, and Through the Key Hole events and let them know Jamie sent you.*

SPOOKY &
THE GHOSTS OF THE RIVERVIEW

The Riverview Hotel, New Smyrna, Florida

Florida's New Smyrna is no stranger to visitors. Situated between Daytona Beach and Cape Canaveral it is a popular tourist destination. The warm weather and charm draw many visitors to the area. New Smyrna's Riverview Hotel, a shining example of the area's hospitality, seems to host guests from both sides of the shroud.

The Riverview

The Hotel's History

The Riverview Hotel is located on the east bank of the Indian River in New Smyrna. It was built in 1885 and was known as The Barber House. It was run by Captain S.H. Barber and his wife (they were also the original bridge tenders). They were at their busiest in the winter months when all the "snow birds" headed south during the colder months.

The original structure was two stories, but in 1910 it was raised up to add another story which would include a lobby and dining room. Then in 1930 the south wing was added for more guest rooms.

The Barbers sold the hotel in 1936 and the name changed to The Riverview Hotel. The new owner, Fred Tryon, had been the head chef at the Alcazar Hotel in St. Augustine, before moving to New Smyrna. He made several changes to the hotel and it was once again only open during the winter months.

During the years of 1941-1945 the hotel opened year round and housed the Coast Guardsmen who patrolled the beach during World War II. Even after the war ended, the hotel stayed very busy, but it wouldn't last. After several failed attempts at re-imagining the place, the hotel sat vacant from 1981-1984. A short time after that The Riverview Partners of Jacksonville became involved with the hotel and it underwent renovations. In 1990, Jim and Christa Kelsey bought the hotel and put a lot of work and love into it. This Victorian style beauty is a landmark in New Smyrna, and a testament to these owners.

Paranormal Tales of the Riverview from the Staff and Guests

Today the Riverview Hotel has another set of owners, but it appears that at least one of the former ones is still lingering. Many people believe that the spirit of Christa Kelsey is still here because of the feeling of love and warmth that is felt when you walk in the front door. Guests describe it as a euphoric feeling that resonates throughout the hotel. Christa had a passion for this historic building and for life. She passed away in 2010 and that is when this supernatural feeling of love and comfort permeated the hotel, especially the lobby and front desk area. Interesting enough, this is also

31

where her photo tribute is placed. I spoke with several employees who worked here when Christa and her husband owned the hotel and have experienced some unusual paranormal activity related to her. They have all claimed, "She's still here."

While doing my interviews it also became very clear from reports by staff and guests that Christa was not the only ghost in the hotel. Adrienne, who works at the front desk, shared several other experiences with me. One night while she was assigned to the front desk there was a male hotel guest sitting on the couch in the lobby. She had her back turned towards him. Out of the corner of her eye she caught a glimpse of the upper torso of a man approaching the desk. She turned around, thinking it was the guest from the couch needing something, and she watched amazed as it vanished in front of her. The male hotel guest was still sitting on the couch completely oblivious to the whole thing.

Adrienne further confided in me that the staircase is also believed to be haunted. While a nearby photo, of Christine, on the staircase area might have something to do with it; Adrienne suggested that this might instead be because of all the people who have come and gone up and down those stairs and through the lobby. "A lot of energy has passed through here in the last 100 plus years and I am sure some of it has stayed with us," Adrienne claimed.

The hotel's handyman Johnny has also had a paranormal experience or two. In one room he claims he saw an apparition of a woman in a white dress. He thought at first it was a co-worker, but as he realized it wasn't her and looked more closely she vanished. On another occasion, while walking through the second floor hallway, he heard the sounds of heavy footsteps. This was hard to believe because he was all alone and the floor is carpeted.

The housekeeping supervisor, Patty, and several other employees don't like going into the attic. One day when Patty went in to get supplies she felt a finger run half way up her back. She turned around and there was no one there and nothing nearby that she could have been bumped into. Needless to say, it spooked her and she left the attic. On another occasion Patty claims she got locked in the attic, a pretty neat trick since the door didn't have a lock on it. Once trapped inside she discovered that she couldn't even turn the door knob. It was as if something were holding it. She had to pry the door open to get out. This has happened to her more than once!

On another occasion while guests were staying in a room on the third floor, they woke up in the middle of the night hearing stomping above them. All that was above them was the building's roof and unless someone or something was on it they shouldn't have heard anything. They demanded to be put in another room. The roof was investigated and there was nothing there. The guests were moved to another room and all was quiet.

The last spirit I want to mention (though there are many more) is Spooky. Spooky was the hotel's black cat and mascot. Spooky passed away in November of 2012, but many people have seen him sitting on the front porch or in the doorways. Some have even reported seeing a small dark image dash across the lobby as Spooky had done many times.

Spooky in her living years
Courtesy of The Riverview Hotel

Our Investigation

Historic Haunts Investigation had the opportunity to investigate the hotel in April of 2013. Unfortunately, we had a very uneventful investigation. If you do enough investigations you realize this happens more often than not. My team retired to their rooms, as did I. After a long and late night all I wanted was a shower and to get some sleep.

I locked my room door, got my things and went into the bathroom. I shut the door and turned the shower on. As I lathered up my hair with shampoo I heard the bathroom door open. I didn't think anything of it, it is an old building. I reasoned I hadn't closed the door all the way. Then, I heard footsteps! I thought, "Oh crap! I didn't lock the rooms front door!" Concerned I peeked from behind the shower curtain and continued to hear the footsteps, but saw nothing. The light above the sink blocked out as the footsteps suggested something passed in front of the spot while walking over to the window. Then judging by the sounds it turned and came back. This phenomenon was followed by the bathroom door shutting on its own! Needless to say this spooked me a bit and I quickly finished my shower. I got the meters and some equipment back out, but nothing more happened. I decided that since it didn't interact, whatever it was must have just been residual energy.

Interestingly enough, just a few nights after my stay, another guest experienced a similar occurrence in the same room.

A few last thoughts about the Riverview Hotel, even though this historic landmark is haunted, it is one of the most relaxing places I have ever stayed, and it's very hard for me to relax (especially while my guard is up looking for paranormal activity after a shower)! It didn't take me long to feel right at home in the place and after the excitement died down, I enjoyed a great night's sleep. Paranormal fan or not, if you visit New Smyrna, and are staying overnight, the Riverview Hotel is a must!

MR. NASTY AND THE GHOST OF LITTLE JESSIE MAY

May Stringer House & Hernando Heritage Museum, Brooksville, Florida

*May Stringer House
& Hernando Heritage Museum*

Do you pay attention to big buildings? While I'm sure the answer would be yes if you were a real estate agent, some of us admire these structures for other reasons. Touring grand and decorative houses is not uncommon, especially old and historic Queen Anne style homes like the May Stringer House in Brooksville Florida. However, when the house that has piqued your interest has drawn the attentions of several in the paranormal field and claims to be one of the most haunted in the state; it's no surprise that this author and investigator wants to research and explore it as well. Upon investigating the May Stringer House in May 2012, I found this beautiful old gem is not only full of history, but also full of ghostly activity.

The May Stringer House History

The May Stringer House (now also known as the Hernando Heritage Museum) was built in 1856 by John May. The original part of the home that he built was actually only four rooms, the parlor and dining room downstairs, and two bedrooms upstairs. All four rooms had their own fireplace and the way the house was built, they all shared one chimney.

John May started a plantation which ended up being the second largest in Brooksville. He died at an early age of tuberculosis in the home and his wake was held in the parlor. He was buried on the property. John's wife, Marena, was left with two little ones, and after his death she stayed in the home for nine years raising the children on her own and taking care of the plantation.

Then Marena met and married Frank Saxon, a Confederate soldier and hero, who had been a prisoner of war at a camp in Atlanta. Unfortunately, not long after they married Marena died during child birth. Before passing she gave birth to a daughter by the name of Jessie May Saxon. Like her first husband John, Marena's wake was also held in the parlor. Marena's daughter Jessie only made it to the age of three before she too fell ill and died in the house as well. Yet another wake was held in the parlor. The family members were buried on the property.

After the May/Saxon family left the home, a physician, Dr. Sheldon Stringer, bought the four room home adding ten rooms for his wife and three children. Besides his residence, Stringer also maintained a doctor's office in the home. The doctor treated many patients here during his time here from 1880 to 1949. Reportedly patients that were too far gone with illness and knocking at death's door were put in the attic room so they wouldn't make his family or the other patients sick. Besides the everyday maladies, the house saw a lot of death from natural causes, diseases, and even witnessed one man who was shot on the front porch.

The house became a rental property for twenty-four years starting in 1950. The rent was only $100, a low rent even for the time. It is believed that this is when many of the ghost stories began to become public.

Perhaps because of the paranormal activity no one seemed to stay there long. By 1978 the building was ready to be condemned and had been abandoned for six years. In 1980 the Hernando Historical Museum Association bought the building and put over $300,000 into renovations to make it the wonderful museum it is today. In fact, it is now listed on the National Register of Historic Places.

Paranormal Reports: Housing History and Active Spirits

The historic May Stringer house has become Brooksville's most popular museum. It has become a home for not only items attached to its former occupants, but to over 10,000 artifacts from different eras and with their own backgrounds and stories. In some cases, these items are believed to have spirits attached to them. In combination with the spirits of the former residents believed to dwell here and on the grounds, that makes the restored May Stringer House a very active paranormal hot spot.

Volunteer Bonnie Letourneau gave us a grand tour of the house before graciously allowing us to investigate. She shared some of the paranormal reports and her personal experiences while volunteering here over the last ten years.

One of the most popular and active spirits encountered frequently at the home is thought to be that of Jessie May Saxon. Bonnie, like many others, has experienced this haunt firsthand. She described hearing the chilling sounds of Jessie May calling for her mother. Bonnie's daughter has even experienced some of the child's activity and doesn't really like to be alone on the second floor. Many people (and even restoration workers) have reported hearing tiny footsteps, children's giggles, seeing moving shadows, and feeling the touch of a tiny hand. She also seems to like to move the toys around in "her" room. She is very fond of the baby in the day bed in the children's room (you never refer to the baby as a doll; she thinks it's her baby and not a doll). She also doesn't like the baby being mistreated. Making either of these mistakes will apparently draw unwelcome activity.

Volunteers at the May Stringer have learned this first hand when they removed the doll from the cradle for an appraisers review. When they later entered the room to return the doll, they found the cradle it rested in disassembled and scattered across the floor, as if someone angrily pulled it apart. The workers reassembled the cradle, placing the doll back in its former spot. There have been no other incidents with the cradle, though Jessie continues to make her presence known in other ways.

In addition to the activity of Jessie May upstairs, tea cups in the dining room downstairs have also been known to vibrate, on their own, and have apparently even completely flipped over in front of a room full of tour guests. Witnesses and volunteers also reported hearing what they described as "old time" music playing frequently, though there are no radios in the room.

35

Another area with common reports of activity is the upstairs hallways. During one of Bonnie's tours a man in his late 30's or early 40's wanted to take a photo of the upstairs hallways and was very persistent about it, even interrupting the tour. Finally, Bonnie pulled him aside and allowed him to take pictures of the upstairs hallway, but only after he told her his story. Which she relayed to us:

As a child, his family had rented the house because of its cheap rent and large lot of rooms. The family went out one night and when they returned home, all the doors and windows were slamming shut repeatedly sounding as if a hurricane were blowing through the second floor. In addition, all kinds of strange noises were coming down the staircase. The father sent his family into the front yard and decided to take the dog and go back in to examine what in the world was going on. As they started towards the staircase the dog got scared and wouldn't go near the steps. He was literally terrified and shaking, that dog had never shown signs of fear before. They were both startled by the sudden sounds of eerie moans coming from the second floor and the "wind" in the house kicking up even harder. This was enough for the frightened family man. He took off outside and left with his family to a friend's house. The next morning they came back, packed all their belongings and moved out.

The man who lived here as a boy just wanted to come back and look at the second floor hallway to see if there was any way possible for those things to have happened on their own. In examining the hallway he confirmed what he already suspected, that it wasn't possible.

Besides the hallway, another active area is upstairs. There is a room on the second floor known as the school room because it contains old artifacts from the local school house. Before its educational ties, when the building was a rental property, a WWII soldier (upon returning home) stayed here for a short while. He wanted to marry the love of his life. She had sent him letters while he was overseas at war. Unfortunately when he returned home he found out that she married another man and he was crushed. He was so distraught that he hung himself in the attic. He is often seen in the îschool roomî because that is where he stayed when he lived here. Police often report seeing a man staring out the school room window at night, when the alarm is set and no one is in the building.

Police have also repeatedly reported seeing a man matching the description of Frank Saxon on the second floor porch. According to volunteer reports he seems to get very upset when people don't show respect to the house and the residents who are here. The Saxon family seems to be seen throughout the home at various times.

Frank's wife Marena is also seen in the home and on the front landing. She has spooked locals many times late at night. Most of these encounters describe seeing a transparent woman in a wispy dress, who turns and disappears.

It's not just the front of the house that seems to have activity. Locals and volunteers (including LeTourneau) claim to experience a lot of activity in the rear of the house, a place they call the "War Room" because of the numerous collected artifacts of every American war. Multiple reports have been made of unexplained tapping of the glass display cabinets, and uniformed busts impossibly flying off their space on the shelves.

There are a multitude of other reports of additional spirits in the house as well (many believed to be tied to Dr. Stringer's patients and the man shot on the porch among others). In fact, I could go on describing other encounters reported on the property. Instead, I want to share the experiences we had during our investigation.

Our Investigation Turns Up Jessie May, Mr. Nasty and More

One of my favorite spirits in the building is little Jessie. During our investigation she seemed to enjoy our Mel Meter Hybrid, which is a piece of equipment we use on paranormal investigations that reads electromagnetic fields and temperatures. The top portion of this meter has colorful lights similar to those on a K2 EMF Meter. As we were setting up equipment in the children's bedroom and were talking to her, she made the lights flicker on and off. The room itself seemed to emanate with a playful spirit.

We moved back downstairs after feeling we'd made a pleasant connection with Jessie May. We were hoping to get activity in the hallway, or dining room. We didn't experience the tea cups, but we did faintly hear "old timey" music described by so many when we played back the recordings. The "War Room" was also fairly quiet for us. So we decided to pull our equipment from the downstairs area and dining room and check out the attic area that was reportedly the haunt of Mr. Nasty.

We continued our investigation setting up equipment in the area where he is known to be encountered the most. We also began to do an EVP session. As we started to ask questions the atmosphere in the room began to change, the temperature started to drop, and the EMF readings started to rise. In fact, the temperature dropped 15 degrees and the EMF rose to a 30.4 when earlier the reading was 0. All meters and equipment were picking up on something. Then we began to see shadow movement with no light source to explain it. The video camera suddenly shut down and would not work, and the still camera died. The room began to feel dark and menacing, we felt threatened! It felt as though someone was getting very angry, like when you walk into a room where two people have been fighting. Suddenly my arm started burning and I somehow knew we needed to leave the attic, NOW! When we got out of the dormer room and on the staircase landing we examined my arm and I had a long deep red scratch from my wrist all the way up to my bicep and my entire arm was burning. As we stood there we felt as though the entity was still very upset with us, and almost as though it was coming towards us. We retreated down to the second floor, but it felt as though there was still a very heavy energy coming down the stairs after us. My husband Deric turned around and said a few very forceful words to Mr. Nasty, he stood up to him for scratching me and asked him what else he wanted since we'd left his space. We felt the energy start to lessen, as if he were slowly heading back to his attic dormer room. Mr. Nasty was withdrawing for the time being, but was not entirely gone.

We went back down to the main floor with our equipment and started sharing our most recent experiences with Bonnie. She was not that surprised. She knows Mr. Nasty has slapped, kicked, and hit several people during her tenure. I was not the first strong and independent woman to anger him and I get the feeling I won't be the last. However, had we stayed in the attic area, I am certain I would have begun to feel ill like the other investigators of the museum.

After all the persistent reports of paranormal activity in the May Stringer House from locals, volunteers, visitors, and police alike, and after my own taste of Mr. Nasty it doesn't take a genius to draw the same conclusion.

This building is 100% haunted no question about it! Day or night! This historic museum is a wonderful stop while in Brooksville and is a haunted must see. It is full of wonderful artifacts, stories, and many many ghosts. You can do a day time tour and on weekends experience the house in a different way with a ghost tour (watch out for Mr. Nasty).This is one of my favorite Historic Haunts.

Authors Note:

While I didn't immediately experience illness from my interaction with Mr. Nasty like some of the other female members of visiting investigation teams, he may still have affected me. The next day following the investigation I blacked out at work. Since then I have been fighting intense migraines (when before I had none) on an almost daily basis. After visits to thirteen doctors the cause of the migraines still leaves them baffled. This may have nothing to do with Mr. Nasty, but it is an interesting and painful coincidence!

A GHOSTLY SOUTHERN ROMANCE
Barnsley Gardens, Adairsville, Georgia

Barnsley Gardens
courtesy of Wikimedia
Commons

A Novel Romance

Godfrey was born in Liverpool, England in 1805, but ambition drove him to the state of Georgia in America in 1824 with only a shilling to his name. Working diligently as a clerk in Savannah, Godfrey met and married the love of his life, a young socialite named Julia Scarborough in 1828. By 1830, hard work, shrewd business moves and the love of a good woman helped make Barnsley very rich in the shipping and cotton trade industries. He became known as one of the 10 most affluent men in the South. To celebrate their accomplishments, Barnsley and his beloved bride set out to build an elaborate and modern Italianate Mansion. The mansion would be surrounded by a beautiful garden with exotic plants and shrubbery, and would provide an idyllic setting for the two avid gardeners and lovers to settle with their six children. Unfortunately, their love nest and the ground it stood on would be tragically cursed from the start.

The Barnsley Curse

In 1845, Godfrey's wife Julia died of a lung ailment and his infant son passed as well. Devastated, Godfrey halted construction, this would only be a temporary delay, as Godfrey returned to the estate in 1846, and claimed that Julia's spirit visited him in the garden, begging him to finish construction on the estate for their children and future generations. The luxurious estate and gardens were still in progress in 1848 when Godfrey moved in with his remaining family. The Barnsleys continued working towards the eventual completion of the estate when the curse again wreaked havoc upon them. In autumn of 1858, Adelaide, Godfrey's second daughter, died in the house, and in 1862 Godfrey's oldest son Howard would be killed by Chinese pirates while he traveled through the orient looking for exotic plants for the grounds. As the curse continued, Godfrey saw his business ventures beginning to fail, and he reportedly sought out psychics, mediums and religious leaders to help lift the curse from the family and the estate.

The Civil War Era and the Barnsley Curse

During 1861-1865, the Civil War raged through Georgia, and the mansion and the gardens were directly in the path of Sherman's March. A battle took place on May 18th, 1864. The estate suffered irreparable damage during the occupation of troops commanded by US General James McPherson. Godfrey's support of the Confederacy during the war left him with a worthless cotton-buying business, an unfinished house, and an estate in ruins. Godfrey's two remaining sons George and Lucian had left to fight for the Confederacy and after refusing to sign an Oath of Allegiance to the

39

Union, immigrated to South America. Godfrey's daughter Julia experienced the death of her husband to a falling tree in 1868. In 1873, Godfrey himself died practically penniless, and his descendants inherited what was left of his romantic dream..

In 1906, a devastating tornado damaged the manor home blowing away the roof. The remaining Barnsleys, including Godfrey's granddaughter Miss Adelaide Saylor were forced to move into the kitchen wing. The family continued to try to make the best of a bad situation, but the curse struck again. In 1935, an intense fight broke out between Addie Saylor's sons Harry and Preston over monies and restoration of the estate grounds. To Harry's surprise, Preston had a pistol and shot him. Harry died in his mother's arms on the grounds in front of his brother.

Ironically, it was the romantic and tragic hardships of the Barnsley family - described by Addie Saylor to her friend Margaret Mitchell - that helped the author draw parallels with her character Scarlett OíHara and ultimately helped lead to the publishing of the most famous of southern romances, Gone with the Wind in 1936.

The Curse is Lifted

In 1942, three years after Margaret Mitchell's book had been made into a Hollywood blockbuster, and nearly 70 years after Godfrey Barnsley's death, the Barnsley property was sold at auction. Not long after this the estate fell into disrepair. The Barnsley's grand dream was soon overgrown with kudzu. Many years later Prince Hubertus Fugger purchased the estate in 1988. Intent on lifting the curse, he brought a Cherokee chief and medicine man to the property. The chief declared the curse over. Prince Fugger spent year's successfully restoring one of the few antebellum gardens in the United States, and expanding these historic gardens to include more than 200 thriving varieties of roses. The Barnsley estate now enjoys new life as the Barnsley Gardens, a resort destination with world class amenities, cottages, golf, restaurants, and a full service spa.

The Haunted Lovers and Other Ghost Stories

There was so much love and sorrow at the Barnsley Resort grounds, throughout its "cursed" history that it's no wonder that some of the deceased may have decided to stay here. Apparitions of Godfrey and Julia have been seen by many different people. Most reports describe a loving couple walking through the beautiful gardens. Most witnesses don't even recognize this couple as out of place until they realize what the couple is wearing (mid-1800's garb) Witnesses only then began to study the couple more closely and realize they were transparent. In fact, by the time most witnesses process this, Julia and Godfrey have disappeared. These paranormal encounters have been described by resort guests so often to employees that they barely pay it any attention. Besides, most of the employees have experienced it themselves!

Other reports of supernatural activity describe more than just the loving couple. With over 200 people believed by some historians to be buried on the grounds, accounts of the paranormal abound. Many of these reports describe shadows, and playfully mocking entities, however, none of the reports detail any threatening or hostile intentions. It seems the ghosts here are just as calm and serene as the picturesque landscape. Overall, the former Barnsley plantation remains a fantastic and romantic Georgia landmark, a source of high-end hospitality and an even better Historic Haunt

PARROTS, SPIRITS AND THE IMMORTAL SIX HUNDRED

Fort Pulaski, Cockspur Island, Georgia

An Ironic History

The White House burned! During the War of 1812, the British sailed up the Potomac and set fire to our most beloved capital building. After the War, President James Madison realized only too well that the threat of foreign invasion required a more rigid system of coastal defense and fortification. After taking control of 150 acres of land on the claw-shaped Cockspur Island (east of Savannah); the

Fort Pulaski interior

government began construction on a fort to better protect this area of the United States. Construction began in 1829 under the direction of Major General Babcock, and continued later under a young Lieutenant Robert E. Lee. Lee had gained a solid reputation as a member of the United States Army Corps of Engineers. His planning and preparations would allow this masonry fortification - described by some as the "mother of all brick fortresses" - to be built on difficult marsh land and soft mud.

In 1833, this fortification was named Fort Pulaski after Kazimierz Pulaski, a Polish soldier and military commander who fought in the Revolutionary War under the command of George Washington. Pulaski, a noted cavalryman, distinguished himself in the sieges of Charleston and Savannah. Like its namesake, Fort Pulaski distinguished itself from other forts with its estimated 25,000,000 bricks and 32 foot high walls (that varied in thickness from 7 to 11 feet). Upon its completion in 1847, after eighteen years and nearly $1 million in construction costs, Fort Pulaski was thought by most to be impenetrable except by the largest land artillery. Since the nearest land was beyond the reach of the artillery of the time, it was assumed the Fort would be invincible. In fact, young Lieutenant Robert E. Lee even remarked, "one might as well bombard the Rocky Mountains as Fort Pulaski"

Historical photo of Parrot guns

"Parrots" and the Battle of Fort Pulaski

From the time of its completion in 1847, until 1860, the Fort was under the control of only two caretakers and housed only 20 of the planned 146 guns. So it was no surprise that the Fort would be seized easily by the State of Georgia under the orders of Joseph E. Brown, Georgia's Governor. Georgia (like South Carolina in 1860) would secede from the United States in 1861, and Fort Pulaski would fall under the control of the Confederate States of America. The Civil War had begun!

41

Confederate control of the Fort would be short lived, however. On April 10th-11th, 1862, Union Forces on Tybee Island would conduct a 30 hour bombardment of the Fort, utilizing the new technology of the "Parrot" Rifle Cannons (named after their West Point creator). These parrot rifles and their explosive shells were easily able to reach the Fort and rendered its brick fortifications obsolete. With these cannons the Union forces broke through one of the corner walls (exposing some of the forts munitions) and in conjunction with large scale amphibious operations, caused the Fort to surrender. Remarkably, only two soldiers -one on each side- were reported to be injured during the battle.

Illustration of the shelling of Fort Pulaski published in Leslie's Weekly

The Aftermath of the Civil War and the "Immortal Six Hundred"

After the battle, the Union troops repaired the damaged wall and took over the Fort causing the South to lose the Savannah port and crippling their efforts during the war. As the battle raged on many atrocities were committed by both sides. In 1864, the Confederate Army used a large number of imprisoned Union Army Officers in Charleston, South Carolina, as human shields against federal artillery. The Union responded in kind by ordering six hundred captured Confederate Officers to be taken to Morris Island, South Carolina and used as human shields against the Confederate gunners of Fort Sumter. These men became famous among the members of the confederacy as the "Immortal Six Hundred". After the captured Union officers were removed from Charleston by the South, the Union transferred the Immortal Six Hundred to Fort Pulaski (now a prison for captured Confederate soldiers). During their time at Fort Pulaski, thirteen of the Immortal Six Hundred would die due to disease and complications from starvation, dysentery and scurvy. The remaining members of the Six Hundred would be sent to Hilton Head Island, South Carolina, and Fort Delaware (gaining further notoriety with a failed escape attempt and refusal to take an oath of allegiance to the Union).

Besides the Immortal Six Hundred, Fort Pulaski would be used as a prison for other noteworthy Confederates and political prisoners, including a Confederate Secretary of State, Secretary of the Treasury, and Secretary of War. After the war, the use of the Fort began to decline. It saw limited use during the Spanish American War in 1898. By the turn of the 20th century it had fallen into disrepair. On October 15th, 1924, the Fort was declared a national monument by order of President Calvin Coolidge. The National Park Service took over in August of 1933 and began repairing the Fort. After a brief stint as a U.S. Navy section base during World War II, it reverted to Park Service Control. It was listed on the National Register of Historic Places on October 15, 1966.

Historical monument to the Immortal Six Hundred courtesy of Wikimedia Commons

Reports of the paranormal

Paranormal reports in places of Historic importance are common, especially in areas that have seen battle. One commonly reported paranormal incident at Fort Pulaski involves the sound of gun shots, often late at night. When the park is closed, people passing by the fort or employees still on the grounds have reported the sound of musket fire from the fort and surrounding property.

Other reports involve witnesses seeing apparitions in the prison area, possibly some of "The Immortal Six Hundred". There is also the sound of movement in that area. People have reported stepping into the cell area and hearing another person in there with them, when they know they are totally alone. Footsteps and the sound of breathing are also reported here, as well as strong sensations of sickness, fear and despair.

Interestingly enough, one report that's hard to ignore came from a group of Confederate soldier "extras" dressed in uniform for the Civil War era movie ***Glory*** (1989). The extras decided to visit Fort Pulaski on the way to the set. They were surprised by the sudden appearance of a Confederate Lieutenant who approached them and reprimanded them. They were ordered to fall in line, which they did as a show for the Fort's other visitors. The officer gave the order to about face before vanishing into thin air.

My Own Pulaski Experiences

I have also had strange experiences while at Fort Pulaski. In one instance, while visiting here and walking through the jail area I saw a shadow. I thought someone had come in behind me, but when I turned around there was no one there. I turned back around and the shadow was still there. I can't cast two shadows.....at least not when one of them is at least a good 5 inches taller than me and with much broader shoulders. The angle of the sun made the casting of two shadows by me impossible. Since I knew there was no one "living" in there with me I started taking photos. As is suggested in paranormal investigations I "bracketed" taking five or six shots of the same area in the same way. The shadow didn't appear in the photos, but in one of the pictures there appears to be a face! The first thought I had when I saw this photo was that matrixing had occurred (when patterns or details looks like something they aren't). However, as I looked closer at the photos and saw that the face was only in one of the pictures, I ruled out matrixing.

I have heard reports of others capturing the same image in that same area so I concluded there must be something to it. In some cases even historical groups or visitors merely taking pictures for posterity with no interest in the paranormal. In fact, there are many reports from tourists and park rangers of seeing shadows in that same area. Whether you visit the Fort to try to capture some type of evidence yourself or just as a tourist, Fort Pulaski is worth a visit. It is a rich piece of history and a haunting reminder of America's past.

GEORGIA
Historic Haunts of the South

THE GHOSTS OF JEKYLL ISLAND
Jekyll Island Club Hotel, Jekyll Island, Georgia

Photo courtesy of the Jekyll Island Club Hotel

The Jekyll Island Club Hotel is haunted! This is one of the more active locations that Historic Haunts Investigations has investigated. We have been here twice and had numerous experiences. Each time we visit we are blown away by the gracious staff, the variety of activities to immerse you in, and the amazing food and drink. We have to remind ourselves we are supposed to be working and not on vacation. Still as paranormal investigators it's not too hard to get back on track, the Jekyll Island Club Hotel seems to offer a lot to explore for fans of the paranormal, and just like it does to the hotel's guests (there is even a local ghost tour).

Before we get into the paranormal activity, let me tell you a little about the history of the buildings that make up the Jekyll Island Club.

The History of the Jekyll Island Club

Newton Finney and his brother-in-law John Eugene DuBignon were the early developers of the club. Ground was broken in August in 1886. What started as a plan for a hunting club for wealthy northerners became a winter retreat for the social elite. At one time it was referred to in a 1904 magazine as "the richest, most exclusive, the most inaccessible club in the world."

The Club was designed by Charles Alexander from Chicago with a Queen Anne style and opened in January 1888. On the outside it featured extensive verandas, bay windows, extended chimneys and a turret that dominated the roof line. On the inside visitors enjoyed its Ionic columns, 12-15 foot ceilings, wainscoting, detailed wood and glass work, and 93 distinctively detailed fireplaces. Over the years the club had more investors including; Henry Hyde, Marshall Field, J.P. Morgan, Joseph Pulitzer, and William Vanderbilt. Besides the extravagant Jekyll Island Club itself, several of the

44

wealthy members built their own retreats on the property. These "cottages" were where some of the elite spent their winters, along with entire families and staff. The cottages were hardly that and in actuality were more like large residences with nods to Victorian tastes and architecture.

In 1892 Indian Mound Cottage was built for William Rockefeller and showcased distinguishing features like an elevator and a cedar lined walk-in safe. The San Souci building was built in 1896 and owned in part by J.P. Morgan. It is considered one of the first condominiums built in the country. The Cherokee Cottage was built for the Shrady family in 1904. The Goodyear cottage was completed in 1906 by the Firm of Carrere and Hastings. Crane Cottage was built in 1917 for Richard Teller Crane Jr. It was the largest and most lavish cottage and featured formal sunken gardens, fountains, and an upper terrace.

Then, there's Hollybourne which is my favorite of the "cottages" separate from the main club building. It was built in 1890 for Charles Stewart Maurice, a well-known bridge builder. Maurice's decision that the Jekyll Island Club accommodations would not suffice led to his building his own home away from home, and may have kicked off the cottage craze as the other socialites did not wish to be out done. During the winters Maurice moved here with his family of eight and employed Charlie Hill who lived on the island during the winter months as well. He was originally the Maurice family's carriage driver.

The Maurices lived at Hollybourne for over 50 years during their winter retreats. In 1942, when the Maurice daughters closed the house down for the final season, Charlie Hill helped them with the tedious task.

The club continued to thrive into the 1930's. However, world events would change that. World War I saw many members offering their yachts to the government for the war effort. Club membership dwindled further with the onset of the Great Depression. By World War II, the threat of enemy subs off the coast induced the evacuation of the island. While the club looked forward to re-opening after the war, the state of Georgia intervened in 1947, buying the island with the intent of making a public state park. Today several club properties are leased from the state of Georgia and these restored and transformed structures make up the luxurious Jekyll Island Club Hotel.

Our First Investigation

The first investigation we did at the Club was in May 2012. We came with only two members of our Historic Haunts Investigation Team, myself and my tech advisor/husband Deric. We were assigned the room railroad magnate Samuel Spencer is known to haunt. Many people have experienced his ghost by having their coffee disappear. Samuel is also known to straighten up or rearrange newspapers that guests leave all over the room. We unloaded our equipment, scattered a newspaper all over the bed and brewed a fresh cup of coffee. We put out a camera and let it record while we went for a late lunch. When we returned to our room, the camera was off, the newspaper was neatly put in order, and more than half the coffee was missing from the cup (certainly more than could be explained by evaporation). We checked the camera and it literally stopped recording as soon as you heard us leave and shut the door.

This was a little frustrating so we turned the camera back on aimed towards the coffee cup and decided we would take a short power nap so we could be fresh before we did any interviews with the night crew to start the investigation. Just as we started to doze off, the camera beeped (as it does when someone turns it off) and the balcony door flew open and then slammed shut! There was neither wind nor anyone on the balcony. Needless to say this startled us and we were both wide awake after that. We figured this was someone's way of letting us know it was time to go ahead and start the interviews and the investigation.

We began by interviewing Patty Henning and Beth Vanderberg, and they shared with us some of the experiences that have taken place in the offices, which are located in the basement. Beth saw a misty figure of a man in her office. He was in late 19th or early 20th century attire and looked quit dapper. He just stood there smiling. He is believed to be Ernest Grob, a former Club super intendant. There is a photo of him in one of the books of photos from the Clubs history and his photo is a dead ringer for the misty figure Beth saw that day. He has also been seen wearing a hat in the area known as Aspinwall.

Between interviews and investigating we took a break on the walking way outside the main lobby. All of the sudden the strong smell of cigar smoke permeated the area. We looked everywhere and there was no smokers nearby, as a matter of fact, there was no one to be seen except one bell boy out on the drive way. We later found out that this happens on a frequent basis and after talking with others at the Club, discovered that perhaps more of them have experienced this than not.

During our interviews we had so many people tell us that the San Souci cottage had a creepy vibe to it that we took a break from investigating the main hotel to go check it out. The security guards we interviewed were a little intimidated by the building. They even told us that they would make a quick run through, completing all their duties and leave as soon as possible once they confirmed all was clear. We were unable to investigate the building thoroughly, but we were able to walk through it and the building does have a completely different feel than the hotel.

We had been told during our interviews that the San Souci had been converted to private suites and that many guests had encountered anomalies or had experiences that creeped them out so badly they checked out in the middle of the night. While walking through the halls of the San Souci we picked up a very strange reading on the K2 EMF Meter (especially on the third floor hallway where it went crazy). We would also get spikes on the staircase, but only in the center of the stairs and at about 4 feet tall. If we moved it left or right, or up or down, the meter would stop. We tried doing a short question and answer session but didn't get any answers. The K2 readings were different than those false readings given by electrical and power sources. In an effort to be thorough, we also tried to discover any electrical sources or other rational reasons why the meter may have gone off and reacted as it did. We found none.

We decided to head back to the hotel and one of the very active locations, the dining room. Sherry, the concierge shared a story with us about a time when she was helping set up for dinner. Sherry and another woman had just completely put out the place settings, glasses, silverware, and had just pushed in the chairs for one table for dinner when they heard piano music. They looked at each other, confirming by their startled looks that they both heard it. The other employee came around the table to where Sherry was standing. They both turned and looked towards the piano and no one was there, but it was playing! The piano in question wasn't the type where you could flip a switch and it would play itself, yet there it was playing. While their backs were turned, they heard something clink behind them. When they turned around and looked back at the table, all the chairs had been pulled out as if everyone that had been setting at the table got up and left. Then the music stopped. Had the two women interrupted a private dinner party?

There are a number of other stories we had heard about haunted happenings at the Jekyll Island Club. We tried to concentrate on the ones mentioned to us most frequently.

One was that a large number of guests and employees at the hotel have reported a party going on late at night in the hotel's outside courtyard. The sound of a lively conversation and clinking glasses, and at least one woman's laugh that has been described as beautiful and entrancing have been reported. When employees check out this party the noise seems to relocate to the veranda. If you move to investigate the veranda the party jumps back to the courtyard. We explored the courtyard and veranda, but didn't encounter this phenomenon and our equipment picked up nothing.

Several other reports detailed a basement hallway near the library where employees felt as if something was behind them looking over their shoulder, and generally making them feel uncomfortable. We explored this hallway and experienced similar sensations. However, we also discovered a large concentration of electrical wiring and other essentials to the hotel that gave off high EMF (Electro Magnetic Field) readings. Typically the readings for these types of areas are continuous, not fluctuating like those suspected around haunted areas. This was the case in the hallway and the sensations described by employees and guests in that area are not uncommon to places with high EMF concentrations.

We also explored the Aspinwall Room, a lovely sun room with a beautiful view where guests of the hotel sometimes enjoy breakfast and where the ghost of General Lloyd Aspinwall has been encountered as well as Ernest Grob, the club's superintendent for 42 years. We explored thoroughly with our equipment and encountered nothing unusual. This was also the case with the DuBignon Room where employees have been shown a guest's photo depicting a transparent woman in 19th century clothing. Our photos and equipment picked up no trace of the woman and only slight activity on our meters of anything else.

We spent the rest of our trip exploring several other areas, but didn't have any experiences on par with those we had witnessed earlier. Unfortunately, our time at this beautiful resort drew to a close. There were too many detailed reports of activity for us to investigate them all. We gathered our equipment and looked forward to returning at a later time.

The frequently "haunted"
Aspinwall Room

Our Second Investigation

In October of 2012, we got another chance. I came with two other members of my team for our second investigation. Although we stayed in a different room (2416) there were similar reports of the balcony door flying open more than once and startling unsuspected guests, and the ghost of a housekeeper named Mini who reportedly still tidys the room. These stories reminded me of my last visit to the hotel. I got the camera set up aimed toward the door, turned it on and it shut off. I tried these four or five times, and every time, it shut itself off. So, I tried another camera and the same thing happened. I took both cameras outside the room and they worked fine.

While on our second investigation we talked with bellmen Rone and Aaron and they shared with us stories about a ghostly bellman who has been seen and heard. Apparently, he is still assisting guests with their luggage and helping them to their rooms. Sometimes when a bellman is pulling the luggage cart to a guest's room they will hear the sound of another cart behind them. They scoot over to one side to allow the other person to pass only to discover there is no one there. Also, when a bellman has luggage loaded on a cart and turns his back for only a few seconds, he will turn back towards the cart and the luggage will be on the floor. This is a common occurrence. Apparently the ghostly bellman has a sense of humor. The apparition of this bellman has been reported and seen multiple times. When he has been seen, he's dressed in 1920's style clothing and is encountered continuing to perform his daily duties. Some guests have even reported having their tuxedo's mysteriously delivered before a wedding.

We investigated the reports of this disembodied bellman, but once again found no trace on our equipment and had no experiences. We also looked into several reports of elevators going up and down on their own, but after witnessing several guests and children pushing buttons before walking away to their rooms or other areas of the hotel, we decided to call this one inconclusive. We looked into other reports and seemed to be experiencing little activity. With so little going on in the Jekyll Island Club Hotel at that time, and recalling some success on our last trip with one of the nearby cottages (San Souci), we decided to branch out and explore another area we heard several stories about, Hollybourne.

According to Stan (one of Jekyll Island's security guards) Hollybourne has reportedly experienced a lot of paranormal activity. There have been reports of black shadows on the roof and many efforts to restore the cottage have been thwarted by malfunc-

tioning equipment and frightened workers. There have even been reports that the building has ïblacked outî areas of photographs not wanting to have its image captured.

We headed to Hollybourne with high hopes and it proved to be the high point of our investigation. We finally got some responses on some of our equipment while outside Hollybourne. They have been trying to restore this building for over

The Hollybourne Cottage

30 years, but whoever or whatever is haunting the halls of this old beauty don't seem to want anyone in their home. We decided to try and do a question and answer session where the side porch used to be. Construction workers at this particular location reportedly don't even last a week here before getting run out by the ghostly inhabitants so we thought we would try to figure out why.

We set our equipment up and started to ask our standard questions. The camera shut off, the digital recorder shut off, and all the meters shut off. We switched out the batteries and tried it again. The same thing happened. Everything turned off and batteries were drained! All we had left was a mini Mag Lite. We figured we would give the flash light test a try. We explained to whoever was there (and draining our batteries) that the flash light was there and all they had to do was tap it for yes and the light would come on. We asked if it understood, and the light came on. Through follow-up questions we found that whoever it is haunting Hollybourne lived here after 1942, but they knew who the Maurice family was. We asked if the spirit wanted the house restored and it said no. We asked if it was worried that people wouldn't do it the way it needed to be done and the flash light replied with yes. We asked a few other questions and got some hesitated responses so we asked, "Do you want us to leave? Make the flash light turn on." The flash light went crazy flashing at us.

We then packed up our gear and thanked the entity for its time. As we started to leave we saw a shadow figure that appeared to be watching us. I darted over to where the shadow was and it went around the building faster than I could get there. When I got to the other side of the building, it was gone. We gathered our gear happy to have gotten some response, but sad to be leaving the next morning.

There are so many stories about the Jekyll Island Club Hotel and surrounding properties, I could write an entire book on the subject (and we still haven't explored it all with two investigations under our belt). None of the members of my investigation team felt anything malicious here at the hotel, just mischievous or perhaps slightly antisocial. Most of the spirits seem playful, curious or eager to act out their habitual behaviors (like most residual haunts). It is a beautiful place to visit and experience rich history, and a peaceful scenic setting. With outstanding amenities and a super friendly staff, you'll see why the Jekyll Island Club Hotel was a seasonal must for the visiting well-to-do. I look forward to another chance to explore this glorious Historic Haunt and the other reports of paranormal activity still to be investigated. I recommend it highly, and if you go, tell them Jamie from Historic Haunts sent you.

THE FABULOUS TWELVE OAKS

Twelve Oaks Bed and Breakfast, Covington, Georgia

Every once in a while a particular historic site I investigate stays with me, holding a special place in my heart and bringing me back pleasant memories. The Twelve Oaks Bed and Breakfast in Covington, Georgia is one of these places. I'm not the only one who appreciates this special area of Georgia. Covington has been a popular location for tourists and cinematographers alike. Movies like **Cannonball Run,**

The Twelve Oaks Bed & Breakfast

Sweet Home Alabama, My Cousin Vinny, Remember the Titans, and **Halloween II** (the recent remake) have all been shot in this area. In fact, the city's nickname is Hollywood of the South. Episodes of the very popular tv shows **Dukes of Hazzard, In the Heat of the Night,** and the current hit **Vampire Diaries** have all been filmed here as well. In some cases episodes have been filmed right at the Twelve Oaks (most recently Vampire Diaries). So what is it about this engaging and endearing area that draws so much attention and makes it so memorable? Perhaps it's the way the area emanates a feeling of historic southern hospitality and charm. If so, then the southern hospitality and charm are perfectly embodied in the gracious and inviting Twelve Oaks Bed & Breakfast.

The Building's Southern Roots

The building that would become the Twelve Oaks was built in 1836 by Judge John Harris as a town home. Harris also owned a large plantation near Covington, but it was pilfered by Federal Troops at the beginning of Sherman's March in 1864.

After the Civil War was over, Robert Franklin Wright bought the property from William Metcalf in 1885 with his wife Salina and they renamed it The Cedars. They refurbished the interior and added the boxwood gardens. This beautiful home sold again in 1903 to Nathaniel S. Turner, a cotton broker who was also the owner of the Covington Mill. He renamed it yet again to Whitehall. As if the mansion wasn't beautiful enough he made major renovations and additions, adding a third floor and a colonnade which accentuated the antebellum look and feel of the home.

The Fabulous Twelve Oaks

Now at 10,000 square feet, this mansion is on the Register of Historic Places and is one of the most stunning locations in Covington. Besides the building being a glorious landmark in Covington and a strong piece of their history, it was also the inspiration to Margaret Mitchell to model Ashley Wilke's home "Twelve Oaks" in *Gone with the Wind* (hence the bed and breakfasts name). If you've seen the movie this would explain why the building would seem familiar to you as you pull up in the drive way.

Our Experiences at Twelve Oaks

Historic Haunts Investigations felt truly honored to be able to investigate here at this amazing mansion in December of 2012. My tech advisor/husband/graphic designer and I headed to Covington to see if we could determine a little more info about the ghosts at this historic bed and breakfast.

Nicole Greer and her son Parker were so gracious welcoming us in and giving us a grand tour of the property. They also shared many of their personal experiences with the ghosts and how a couple of times, construction workers during renovations were so creeped out, they left the job site!

Nicole had told us that one day her fiancé, John Munn, was in the house and heard footsteps upstairs and thought it was Nicole walking around. As he heard the movement above, he also heard a car pull in the driveway. It was Nicole. Believing that he and Nicole were the only ones home, he ran upstairs to see who was walking around in the house. He found no one.

As Deric and I toured the property on our own and were obtaining base readings of EMF (electromagnetic field) and temperature amounts; we heard footsteps following us around the rose garden and near the pool. I stopped quickly as soon as I heard them and catching whatever entity was following us by surprise, we heard one more step after we stopped. This happened numerous times as we stopped abruptly and tried to discover who was dogging our heels. No one was there, but the footsteps repeated. We decided to continue our investigation inside.

We had researched some of the ghost stories involving the Twelve Oaks before we arrived. Many people for decades have reported seeing "The General" on the 2nd floor balcony and peering out the 3rd floor windows. I wondered how people knew he was a general and from what locals said, he appears in such detail you can clearly see he is a Confederate General. Details and information on this were hard to unearth. I was unable to uncover any details of a General that died in or occupied the home. Spirits do occasionally attach themselves to nearby areas, and sometimes to items. Nicole had acquired some items for the bed and breakfast at estate sales, antique shops, or auctions. Perhaps there was a connection.

We thoroughly researched the first two floors of the house (trying not to interfere with the other guests at the Bed and Breakfast). We discovered nothing unusual; readings were normal on our equipment, from all furniture and items and we experienced no paranormal activity. We decided to concentrate our efforts on the third floor where renovations and the presence of construction workers were reportedly stirring something up.

During our first attempt to investigate the third floor, all the new batteries died immediately, as soon as we began. I check every piece of equipment multiple times before we do an investigation and make sure everything is in working order. It's not unusual for investigators to sometimes encounter this phenomenon, sometimes the spirits present pull the energy from devices, sometimes they don't want to be filmed or recorded, and other times you might get a pack of bad batteries (that's why we try to mix up various new packs when we do this). We replaced all batteries with another set of new ones and attempted to investigate again.

Our Conversation with the Lady

Our second attempt on the third floor was a great success. We set the camera up, the digital recorder, and a flash light and began. We had a flashlight session with an entity who we believed to be the wife of the General. She turned on the flash light for a yes response to many questions. We asked if she knew who people referred to as the General and she said yes, then we asked if it was her husband and she replied with yes again.

During our 45 minute Q&A with "the lady of the house" as we referred to her (one of the longest I have ever had with any entity), I felt a great sense of sorrow and heart break and knew that it had to do with a child. I asked her what happened to her baby boy and the flash light got very faint. I suddenly felt hot all over yet cold at the same time and asked if she had lost him. The flash light turned on yet again responding with a yes. I told Deric I felt that he had died of a severe illness and felt as though I had a fever. As soon as I said this, the light came on again. (The following day while doing research on the Twelve Oaks we would learn that in the early 1860's a baby boy had died of the fever in the home)

While we talked with the spirit on the third floor we asked if she knew who William Tecumseh Sherman was and the flash light went nuts turning itself on and off repeatedly. We asked if she was scared during his march through Georgia and she replied flashing yes several times. We assured her he wasn't coming back and the flashlight stopped.

Continuing, we asked her how she felt about the renovations and if she liked Nicole, Parker, and John and she seemed very pleased with them and the renovations. We also asked if she was the one who had scared off a few construction workers and she admitted it was her. Deric said, "We know you didn't mean to do it," and she once again indicated this with the lighting of the flashlight.

As the session went on we noticed her answers were getting weaker and we asked if she was getting tired, she said she was. We thanked her for her time and wished her a good night and the light flashed one more time, and then went out. As we gathered our equipment we were thrilled to discover that unlike the last time, the camera and the digital recorder had been running the entire time.

The following morning we shared some of the highlights of our "illuminating" conversation on the third floor and of the investigation with Nicole and Parker. Parker was happy to learn that the spirits there liked them. We finished an amazing breakfast and friendly conversation with our fellow guests. We packed our gear, and headed back to Florida, sad that our stay at this magnificent place hadn't been longer.

When we returned home I looked forward to reviewing everything from the investigation. I plugged in the digital audio recorder, and was able to play back and confirm the mystery footsteps we encountered in the garden.

Unfortunately, when I got to the video footage of the Q&A session on the third floor

I discovered something was wrong. You could see and hear us setting things back up in the room and stating where we were on video, but after that the video footage seems to have been affected, appearing blank.. The counter continued to count though, and at the end of the session you could hear us saying thank you and leaving. It was as if the question and answer session video had all been erased. Maybe she just doesn't want to be recorded; I guess I might be that way too if I were her. This wouldn't be the first time, and I wouldn't be the first paranormal investigator to encounter entities "unwilling" to be captured by equipment.

Reflecting back on our visit, I know that whether you visit the Twelve Oaks for the history, the beauty or the ghosts, you will love the place. The rooms are exquisite, the breakfast is amazing, and the owners are wonderful people to chat with. I can't wait to go back and visit with them and the resident spirits. Maybe next time I'll bring more equipment and more batteries! I can't wait to go back. To me, this place is Covington's #1 Historic Haunt.

THE BRIDE OF CUMBERLAND FALLS

Cumberland Falls State Park, Corbin, Kentucky

Scenic Cumberland Falls at Cumberland Falls State Park

Water is an amazing conductor of electricity, of paranormal energies, and of interest, especially when it takes the form of a waterfall. Little Niagara is a large waterfall located in Corbin Kentucky at Cumberland Falls State Park. Also known as Cumberland Falls or the Niagara of the South, this 68 foot tall, 125 foot wide waterfall flows with an amazing 3,600 cubic feet per second of water.

There are many things that make this region and this waterfall unique. The waters of this area of the Cumberland River are reportedly a haven for monster size catfish (in some accounts the size of small cars). The falls themselves have two distinctions as well. The first is that Cumberland Falls is the only place in the Western Hemisphere to witness an elusive lunar rainbow or "moon bow". This phenomenon occurs only under full moons and with clear skies, and is formed by the mist from the falls combining with the natural moonlight. To the viewers it appears as an arch of white light that emanates from the base of the falls. According to many residents and visitors in the area the moon bow is tied into the areas second distinction, namely that Cumberland Falls is haunted!

The legends

Back in the 1950's a bride and groom went to Cumberland Falls for their honeymoon. The happy couple walked and laughed along the trails taking in the view of the falls. As they walked the trails they were snapping memorable photos of their happy occasion, and they came upon a truly beautiful view of the falls. The loving groom wanted to take a photo of his beautiful bride with the falls in the background and as she backed up, she stepped just a little too far, and fell to her death. Needless to say the groom was devastated and mourned the loss of his new bride for a long time after her death. The area is now referred to as "Lover's Leap".

In another account of this tragic story the bride was waiting for her groom at the lodge where the wedding was to take place. The groom was thought to be running terribly behind. It was only hours later that the bride discovered that he had been killed in a car crash. Completely inconsolable, the bride-to-be threw herself off the falls in full wedding attire.

54

Whichever version of the story you leans towards, multiple paranormal accounts would seem to indicate the ghostly bride of Cumberland Falls is very real!

The Bride of the Mists

Many people have reported seeing a woman in a 1950's era wispy white dress in the area of Lover's Leap staring at the waterfall. She appears very sad and lonely and the people who have seen her are filled with great sorrow. Other people have also reported seeing her walking up the path towards the falls. She is usually described as transparent or misty in form.

Other eyewitness accounts, including some by park Rangers describe the bride hovering or floating on the water's surface, gesturing to those who see her to join her in the water of the falls. Many believe she is the reason for the unusual moon bows that appear to the curious on moonlit nights.

There are even reports that indicate she may leave the area of the falls. There have been a number of incidents described by guests and state employees at a nearby lodge. Most of these involve apparitions of the bride, moving objects, and the sudden closing and opening of doors. Some employees reportedly refuse to enter certain areas of the lodge.

If you visit the lodge you may encounter the bride yourself. If you're still curious and bold enough to seek her out, her gesturing form may appear to you as you approach the falls near the mists of Lovers Leap. Even if you don't experience the legend at Cumberland Falls it is still well worth the trip seeing the magnificent falls and possibly the ethereal light of a moon bow, the ghostly mist of which might be a sign that the bride is watching you too.

THE GHOSTS OF WAVERLY HILLS

Waverly Hills Sanatorium, Louisville, Kentucky

There is no shortage of haunted locations for those interested in the paranormal to investigate. Few, however, can match the legendary status achieved by Waverly Hills Sanatorium in Louisville Kentucky. It has been featured on multiple paranormal television shows and specials, investigated by a multitude of ghost hunting groups, and been the subject of many stories in urban legends. This has made it hard at times to separate fact from fiction, but many locals, psychics, and paranormal investigators agree on the fact that the sanatorium has a startling history and is very haunted!

*Waverly Hills Sanatorium
courtesy of Wikimedia Commons*

The Sanatorium's Early History

The land that would eventually house Waverly Hills Sanatorium was purchased by Major Thomas Hays in 1883. Lacking a school for his daughters to attend, he built one. He hired Lizzie Lee Harris as the teacher, she intern named the one room school house The Waverley School (after Walter Scott's Waverley novels). Major Hays liked the name and began calling his property Waverley Hills. When members of the medical community in Jefferson County bought the land from Major Hays in the early 20th century to build a treatment area for tuberculosis patients they kept the name (although the spelling changed).

An outbreak of tuberculosis had ravaged Louisville in the early 1900s. In an effort to contain the ìearly casesî of the disease a two-story wood sanatorium was erected with the main building and two open air pavilions that each houses twenty patients. By 1911, the disease was progressing and hospital commissioners of the Louisville City Hospital gave the Board of Tuberculosis Hospital money to build a facility for advanced cases of the disease. A hospital for these pulmonary tuberculosis patients was open in 1912 with room for forty patients. A children's pavilion was added in 1914 with another fifty beds.

As the disease continued to spread to epidemic proportions the need for a larger facility with more beds and requiring fewer repairs became evident. Construction began in 1924. A modern, gothic style building was opening in October 1926 with room for more than 400 patients. This new Waverly Hills Facility was extremely self-sufficient with a post office, water treatment facility, gardens for fruit and vegetables, and farms for meat and livestock. A tunnel was also constructed beginning with the first floor to the bottom of the hill. It had two sides, one with steps to allow working to enter and exit, and the other had a set of rails and a cart with a motorized cable system to bring supplies and gurneys back and forth.

A Note about Sanatoriums and Waverly Hills

At this time in history tuberculosis was known to be a serious contagious disease. îSanatoriumsî were thought to be the best treatment options. Because most medical authorities thought patients needed to be isolated from the general public and places in areas with plenty of fresh air to stay calm and rest; sanatoriums were typically built on hills or higher areas with a scenic atmosphere and peaceful woods to help speed recovery and keep morale high.

Waverly Sanatorium had an extremely dedicated staff. In fact, because of the contagious nature of TB most of these doctors and nurses said good bye to the outside world and committed to living their lives on site. Ironically, doctors of the time had no idea that TB was an air born sickness and while they sequestered themselves, friends and family members of the patients came and went on "visitor days". Still, the staff at the modern Waverly tried many unique and experimental techniques to try and heal their patients.

These treatments were sometimes brutal, causing extreme pain during and after procedures, and often leaving horrific scares or disfigurements. Techniques varied from the fairly innocent "heliotherapy" (exposing patients to extreme rays of sunlight often used on the children on the rooftop) to the potentially deadly "pneumothorax" (surgically collapsing or deflating a portion of the lung so it would heal, fewer than 5% reportedly survived). The staff at Waverly learned that it was less demoralizing to their living patients if they removed the dead discreetly down the hill via the tunnel to hearses waiting below.

Waverly continued treating patients. By 1943, TB was thankfully on the decline due to advancements in antibiotics. There was no longer a need for such a large hospital. The remaining patients were moved to Hazelwood Sanatorium in Louisville. The sanatorium officially closed in 1961. It was quarantined, renovated, and reopened in 1962 as Woodhaven Geriatric Center. Unfortunately, this facility was also closed in 1982 by court order due to patient neglect.

Several attempts were made to repurpose and reimagine the facility in the subsequent years. There were unsuccessful attempts to turn the structure into a prison, apartments, and a chapel that would have contained the world's tallest statue of Jesus on its site.

In 2001, Tina and Charlie Mattingly bought the building. They began restoration projects and started historical and ghost tours to raise more money for the renovations. Obviously the building has a lot of stories to tell, and is definitely not lacking in the ghost department. In fact there have been so many reports of paranormal experiences it's hard to list them all here. The building consistently seems to manifest activity. This comes as no surprise since the death toll from Waverly has been estimated to be anywhere between an unrealistic high of 63,000 and a more likely 8,000.

KENTUCKY

Historic Haunts of the South

Waverly's Paranormal Activity

Waverly has a laundry list of paranormal activity. From reports of specific activity in specific locations to general activity encountered throughout the building and the grounds. The common reports of paranormal activity read like an investigator's check list: footsteps, disembodied voices, screams of pain and wailing, cold spots, light anomalies and orbs, strange moving mists, doors opening and slamming shut, people being touched, shadows and moving shapes seen, and full blown apparitions seen moving throughout the building are frequently captured on film, digital cameras, and infrared technology. A majority of these encounters seem to occur on the very active fourth floor, but some of the more unusual reports come from a variety of other areas in the building.

People for years have also seen what they thought was their reflections in windows, but upon examining the windows find there is no glass present to capture a reflection. Often times at night when staring up at Waverly Hills, lights are seen moving throughout the hospital when no one is in the building, and usually in sections where there is no electricity!

An apparition of a homeless man and his dog are believed to be seen in different places in the building as well. The man reportedly entered the abandoned building with his white dog seeking shelter. Sometime after his death their bodies were found. Many reports state that the imprints of where their dead bodies laid for so long can still be seen in the floor where they died.

And of course there are the stories of more specific rooms in the building...

Waverly's Legendary Haunts

One story comes from the children's wing. If you go on a tour or get to do an investigation here, make sure you bring a ball with you. A male child's apparition has been spotted playing in the hallway. If you bring toys with you the boy's spirit interacts with the toys and sometimes with the living. The apparition appears to be less than four feet tall and has been captured on a thermal camera. It has also been seen in a shadow form. The boy is not the only child encountered at Waverly.

The spirit of a little girl has often been reported on the third floor. Some frequent visitors to Waverly have named her "Mary". Mary likes to play hide and seek with visitors and enjoys peering out third floor windows. Several unsettling accounts detail visitors or guides who have encountered her with no eyes!

Another unsettling location at Waverly is the tunnel that runs beneath it. Nicknamed the "Body Shoot" or "Death Tunnel" this area is reported by many to feel very creepy. Voices are heard and shadows have been seen moving. There have also been reports of the mechanized sounds of the gurney that once carried the dead down to the waiting hearses below.

Of all the rooms at Waverly, perhaps the most infamous is 502. Room 502 is said to be one of the most haunted in the entire building. The legend attached to this room claims that in the 1930's a nurse hung herself in this room. She was unwed and had given birth (in those days that was a big disgrace). Before she hung herself, as the story goes, she threw the newborn baby's body down an abandoned well. When her body was pulled down and examined, it was discovered that she had recently given birth. A search turned up the unfortunate remains of the baby.

There are other variations of this story, but a nurse is always the subject. What makes this more interesting is that it is the full body apparition of a nurse that is so often encountered in this room. Witnesses describe an unsettling feeling accompanying her appearance and several instances of her asking them angrily to get out.

If you are pregnant, I would highly suggest (as a precaution) that you do not enter room 502. Why take a chance on going in there? I'm not saying you are going to hang yourself or that the spirits are going to harm you, but why risk it? Besides, ghost hunting while pregnant is not exactly the smartest thing in the world. Some people believe that when a woman is pregnant; nearby spirits can attach themselves to the unborn child. I don't know if this is true or not, but please don't put yourself or your baby at risk.

Several of Waverly's residents are thought to be tied not to its days as a TB facility, but to its brief incarnation as Woodhaven Geriatric Center. I spoke with a woman who was a candy striper during that time. She said that the conditions at the center were so bad it terrified her at times. One day she came in and an elderly woman, a patient, was sitting in a corner naked and wouldn't speak to anyone or even eat. She also claimed patients would roam around with no guidance only to be abused or screamed at later for not being in their rooms.

Coincidentally, another one of Waverly's more famous ghostly residents is the ghost of an old woman encountered on the buildings lower levels. She appears with restraints around her arms or legs that appear to be drawing blood. She has been heard to exclaim that a friend of family member will be there any minute to pick her up. She moves around excitedly before disappearing. Investigators suggest that this intelligent haunt doesn't realize she has passed on. Most startled visitors don't seem to be in a hurry to let her know.

Waverly Hills Sanatorium is one very intriguing and haunted building. It has become known as one of the "most haunted" hospitals in the eastern U.S. While much of the hype regarding this building might be due to urban myth and exaggeration, there is no denying the incredible number of paranormal reports attached to it. Chances are if you visit Waverly you will encounter some kind of haunted activity. Even if you don't experience something paranormal, the building has a vibe to it that no other place has. As far as I am concerned Waverly Hills will always be one of my favorite Historic Haunts.

GHOSTS OF THE HOTEL MONTELEONE

Hotel Monteleone, New Orleans, Louisiana

New Orleans grand Hotel Monteleone

Who doesn't love an American success story? New Orleans' Hotel Monteleone is an inspiring example of one man coming to America and realizing his dreams. Situated on Royal Street – thought by many to be the grandest street in the French Quarter- this 15 story jewel has garnered awards and wide spread attention for its old world charm, gilded details, and history both natural and supernatural.

A Historic Testament to Entrepreneurial Spirit

Antonio Monteleone has a history of success before he moved to New Orleans from Sicily in 1880 and opened a Cobbler Shop on Royal Street. He was an accomplished shoe factory operator before the lure of adventure in the land of opportunity drew him to the United States. New Orleans, America's most European city, and commerce and banking thoroughfare, seemed a good place to start.

In 1886, Antonio purchased The Commercial Hotel, which consisted of only 64 rooms and had been occupied by Union Troops during the Civil War. Since that time four generations of Monteleones have weathered storms and other hardships dedicating themselves to improving and making this historic hotel a gem of the French Quarter. Five major renovations have been made to the hotel over the years, shaping it into what today is considered one of the last great family owned and operated hotels in America.

The Hotel's first renovation occurred in 1903. Thirty rooms were added to the Commercial Hotel taking its total to 94. Then in 1908, a second renovation was executed, 300 more rooms were added and the name was changed to the Hotel Monteleone. In 1913, Antonio passed away and his son and successor Frank took over and added another 200 rooms in 1928. It was one of the few family hotels that weathered the great depression.

The late 40's and early 50's saw a fourth round of renovations that razed most of the original building. The foundation was laid for a complete new building that would include ballrooms, lounges, dining rooms, and other rooms for special events. In addition, one of the hotel's most famous features was added the Carousel Bar and Lounge. This twenty-five seat feature is the only revolving bar in New Orleans, completing

60

The Carousel Bar
courtesy of Wikimedia Commons

one rotation every fifteen minutes and over-looking Royale Street and the French Quarter. It was also during this time the lounge was the home to the ìSwan Roomî a night club where the likes of Louis Prima and Liberace performed and partied.

Frank passed away in 1958, and his son Bill took over. It was under his direction that the hotel underwent its fifth renovation in 1964. More rooms were added and a sky terrace with a swimming pool and cocktail lounge became signature features of this amazing landmark.

Today's Hotel Monteleone carries on as the largest hotel in the fabulous French Quarter. It was a popular and inspiring place to writers like Tennessee Williams, William Faulkner, Ernest Hemingway, and Truman Capote. Its Carousel Bar has been named one of the best in America by Esquire Magazine (and ironical-ly enough to this author is a favorite filming spot for paranormal themed tv shows and movies). Each year the hotel houses a number of guests and numerous celebrities drawn to the beautiful interiors and rich past of this celebrated hotel. However, it's the hotel's other "guests"and the ghostly reports by visitors and employees that have drawn the attention of various paranormal groups and investigators.

Spirited Employees and "Resident Guests"

With over one hundred years to its credit it's no surprise that the Hotel Monteleone has seen many visitors and characters pass through its doors. What may be surprising is that many of its frequently reported paranormal encounters involve former employees.

One of the ghosts still haunting this grand hotel identifies himself as "Red". He is a middle aged man who was an engineer for many years at the hotel. Apparently he is often seen throughout the hotel repairing things as he did when he lived. He doesn't interact very much with the living, but he will nod his head in acknowledgement to you if you see him and he sees you. He may or may not be the spirit occasionally seen (day and night) working on the antique clock in the hotel lobby. Further, he is believed by some to be behind another report of activity that occurs in one of the hotel's restaurants.

The Hotel Monteleone houses three of New Orleans' finest dining establishments. *Le Café* located on the first floor is among the most active. A ghostly doorman report-edly frequently opens and closes the doors for guests and staff members (sometimes aided by "Red"). If one of the wait staff comes through with their hands full of plates the door will open on its own as if the doorman was there to help. A woman explained to me how she was trying to carry her infant child and hold her little girl's hand and the door opened on its own allowing her into the café. *Le Café* has magnetic locks and the staff is still baffled by the occasional opening of the locked doors. This phenome-

61

non has been captured by investigators on tape usually between 7p.m. and 8p.m. or when someone needs help getting in.

While employees and guests of the hotel often describe encounters with "Red" or at *Le Café* others speak of a spirit dubbed "Ms. Clean". This entity is believed to have been a 4th generation maid who worked at the hotel. She is often experienced following behind housekeeping making sure rooms are cleaned to her satisfaction. She frequently moves the soap in rooms and many guests have woken up in the middle of the night to sounds of running water coming from the bathroom. When they investigate they find the sink and bathtubs completely dry, but the bathrooms smell strongly as if they had been just cleaned. So intent is Ms. Clean on making sure guests have a pleasant stay she has even been known to tuck in guests.

Besides the ghosts of former employees the Hotel Monteleone seems to be a home to former guests who have long since cast off their mortal coils. John Wagner is one of these resident ghosts. He was frequently in New Orleans on business from Tennessee. In life he always seemed to get involved in what seemed like good business deals only to have them collapse after costing him a lot of money. After seeing enough bad business ventures fail he reportedly took his own life at the hotel. His spirit is often seen with a light colored business suite from the 1920's or 30's. Some witnesses suggest that he is still here at the hotel because he feels that he cannot move on due to his suicide. He is often referred to as "Silent John".

Mr. Wagner is not alone though. Another spirit here has been identified as William Wildemere. He died in the hotel of natural causes, but loved the hotel so much in life that he has returned, or perhaps never left. Most witnesses describe seeing him out of the corner of their eye. When they turn to look back at him, he is gone. Recently a friend of mine stayed at the Hotel Monteleone while she and her husband were in New Orleans. They actually encountered Mr. Wildemere three different times during their five night visit.

The 14th Floor and the Roof Top Lovers

Like many hotels in various parts of the world superstitions cause builders to rename the 13th floor. In this case the Hotel Monteleone's "14th floor" is known to be the most paranormally active. It is believed to be haunted by the spirits of several small children who like to play hide and seek. Guests frequently report hearing giggling, and the sounds of little feet running, and experiencing sudden and freezing cold. One of these child spirits is believed to be young Maurice Begere. The boy, while alive, had been feeling ill and was left with a nanny while his parents visited the opera. The boy had a convulsion and died unexpectedly. He has been described by guests appearing at the foot of their beds and mischievously throughout the 14th floor.

Guests have also reported the appearance of two lovers. A young woman made a suicide pact with her boyfriend at the roof top bar. As she started to question what they agreed upon and wanted to tell him she changed her mind the pact was fulfilled. She was shocked and grieved the loss of her love. While the man's spirit doesn't return often, apparently she does and is still grieving at the roof top bar near the pool. People have reported seeing and hearing a woman crying near the ledge where he jumped.

The Mardi Gras Streaker and the rest

There are a variety of other paranormal reports throughout the hotel. Some describe the ghost of a Mardi Gras reveler encountered in several rooms naked except for his mask. He is usually encountered streaking through rooms excitedly before disappearing into thin air. However he is not the only Mardi Gras related ghost. Other guests have described being serenaded by a ghostly jazz musician. Additional reports by other hotel guests describe seeing human like figures in some of the hotel's claw foot chairs. Occasional balls of light have even been captured in the elevators by security cameras.

The Hotel Monteleone is obviously extremely active. In fact in March 2003, the Internationally Society of Paranormal Research (ISPR) spent several days investigating and reported making contact with more than a dozen earth bound entities none of which were malevolent. The hotel is considered one of the ten most haunted hotels in America, and has been featured on Weird Travels on the Travel Channel and Spirits of the South. Some have even said that it is the best place to begin exploring New Orleans, even noting that "the French Quarter begins in the lobby of the Hotel Monteleone". Whether you find yourself in the Big Easy for a night or a week, I recommend this amazing landmark hotel. It is full of rich architecture, history and is truly one of New Orleans Historic Haunts.

THE NEW ORLEANS DEVIL BABY
New Orleans, LA

Have you ever been afraid of a doll? Many horror movies depict dolls which move and react on their own. Whether the stuff of nightmares or cinema, some of these stories seem to be based on frequent eyewitness accounts. One of the most popular and unnerving is the Devil Baby of New Orleans.

The Legend of the Devil Baby

There is a New Orleans legend about the "Devil Baby" which has been told for many years. It was a deformed child of a Creole doyenne with monstrous features who was adopted by the Voodoo Queen Marie Laveaux and christened by Madame LaLaurie. Until its death, the infant reportedly terrified the residents of the French Quarter and nearby neighborhoods from the shadows of its alleys and old city streets. Many residents believe the tiny bones of this baby are buried with its adopted mother Marie Laveau in St. Louis Cemetery #1.

While the child lived, people inhabiting the French Quarter created their own "devil babies" by carving gourds to resemble the poor deformed child. They thought hanging them in their windows would keep the actual child away by scaring it. Other carved dolls appeared on the doorsteps of voodoo targets. These original dolls are very rare and have mostly been passed down through the generations of the original families who owned them. They were most often fashioned with horn and a tail.

During the early 20th century newer versions of the Devil baby doll starting popping up around New Orleans. These dolls were made with glass eyes and horns coming out of the foreheads. They reportedly looked more like the actual baby did, wearing clothing and were able to stand on their own limbs unlike the original dolls. Bad luck seemed to follow the owners of these dolls. It was said that Marie Laveaux placed a curse on them.

The Devil Baby Rises Again

The devil baby dolls are being recreated yet again by a modern day artist with exacting details from a recovered original. Apparently these handmade dolls have taken on lives of their own and seem to have an element of the supernatural about them. They have been known to move on their own and have even relocated themselves when they desire. Many people have claimed that their eyes follow you when you move about the room, and that when gathered together the dolls rustle around and whisper with one another.

The artist tried to convince a few of his friends to keep the new version of the dolls and almost immediately, the haunted happenings continued. Many of the artist's friends decided they no longer wanted to house the dolls when they discovered they had moved themselves, and that things were disappearing. The dolls have even been known to hide in closets or rearrange things in a room. Other doll owners claim to hear crying, and baby noises and report that their animals are terrified of the dolls. Some people believe these dolls were just "born" with a dark soul.

It's hard to know the truth behind the Devil Baby. Maybe this is just a sad story about a poor child blown out of proportion or maybe it's just typical New Orleans!

THE LADY IN BLACK
Oak Alley Plantation, Vacherie, Louisiana

The "Oak Alley" to the main house

"In the beginning...." there were trees! At least that is what they like to tell you when giving some background of the fabulous Oak Alley Plantation in Vacherie, Louisiana. These trees, some of them over 300 years old, mark the quarter mile walk way and distinct entrance to the "Big House" of this beautiful plantation. It's unforgettable view is a striking study at times in both romantic elegance and eerie etherealness. Movies like **Hush Hush Sweet Charlotte** and **Interview with a Vampire** have put its now famous tree lined image on display, and history buffs and authors (like myself) can't help wanting to write about it.

The Romantic Oak Alley

It is believed that Canadian born Michael Arceneaux was the first owner of the property now known as Oak Alley Plantation in 1704. He planted 40 live oak trees on the property, most between the house and the river (creating the alley) and a small four room home to live in.

The present day mansion was built between 1837 and 1839 by wealthy Creole sugar planter Jacques Telesphore Roman and his wife Celina. He built his home here because of the proximity to the Mississippi River. The twenty-eight oak trees lined the driveway that led straight to the river. Celina called her prized plantation "Bon Sejour", but the riverboat captains later dubbed it "Oak Alley" and the name stuck.

The Roman family was originally quite wealthy from the sugar industry. The plantation carried on successfully until Jacques Telesphore died from tuberculosis in 1848. His widow went on spending freely in the heights of Creole society. Her only surviving son Henri, took over family affairs in 1859. He tried valiantly to maintain the family's wealth and interests, but the Civil War and post war issues forced the family to sell the plantation in 1866 for $32,800.

The plantation changed hands several times between 1866-1925 until Andrew and Josephine Stewart purchased the plantation and restored the home to its original glory. Josephine took pride in the home and after her death she left the plantation as a non-profit foundation so many others for years to come could appreciate the history and beauty of the property.

Historic Haunts of the South

The Plantation's Ghosts and the Lady in Black

With such a long history attached to the land and home, it's no surprise to learn that there are a lot of spirits attached to it. One tour guide shared with us that a group of over 30 tour guests saw a candle fly across the room. Apparently the spirit wasn't expecting such a large group and was unhappy about the unannounced arrival. Whenever several people see or experience the same thing at the same time those in the paranormal field refer to it as a collective sighting. With more than one person experiencing something paranormal at the same time; these types of phenomenon are more credible than those of a single witness. They are usually rare, but seem to occur frequently at Oak Alley.

Many at Oak Alley have reported hearing the clip clop and seeing the dust kicked up by an ethereal horse drawn carriage. There are also îtypicalî paranormal reports of people being touched by unseen hands, a child's cry echoing through the mansion, strange flickering lights (baffling even the electrician,) and moving objects. In addition, the property boasts several reports by tour guides and guests of a variety of apparitions (another rarity).

A male apparition all in gray and wearing riding boots has been seen in the kitchen. He doesn't seem to interact with anyone but does vanish right in front of people. His heavy footsteps can also be heard on the first floor. Some suspect him to be the ghost of Mr. Stewart.

Mrs. Stewart's ghost has also been seen in great detail (allowing comparison with pictures on site and positive identification). She is most often encountered gazing from the bedroom by staff and visitors though she has made appearances on the bed and in the kitchen as well. Like Mrs. Stewart Celina Roman's ghost is often seen staring out the windows (in period clothing). She reportedly peers out the windows of the French doors towards the alley as if she is expecting someone to arrive. Perhaps she is looking for the presence of the plantation's most famous spirit, the lady in black. This entity has been spotted strolling among the alley of oaks on property and in several places throughout the mansion. The most famous evidence of her appearance occurred when a touring couple captured her image in a photo. She appeared on a headless dress form in the photograph, but cast no corresponding reflection in the mirror. This image is on display for the curious. It has been suggested that the lady in black might be Louise Roman, eldest daughter of Jacques Telesphore Roman.

My Oak Alley Experiences

Many people including myself have been touched in the mansion. While standing at the top of the staircase, I felt a hand on my right shoulder, I turned around to see who was there and what I saw surprised me. There was no one directly behind me, but there was an apparition of a woman at the foot of the stairs entering the room just to the right. She was transparent and wearing what appeared to be a long light colored night gown. She had long hair pulled back off her face. She entered the room, and as she did I moved down the steps to get a closer look. When I got to the doorway, the apparition was gone there was no one there.

Another personal experience I had was while standing on the upstairs terrace. I was looking through the doorway into the house when I heard the sound of a horse and carriage coming down the alley behind me. I thought, fantastic! A great photo opportunity since I am an amateur photographer. But, when I turned around, there was no horse and carriage to be seen. As I studied the alley wondering if there was any place the ghostly carriage could have disappeared to I did see something of interest. There was a woman out on the alley, about eight trees away. She crossed the alley and disappeared behind the ancient oak trees. Later while talking with one of the tour guides I asked him about ghosts and he said people have heard the cloppity clop sound of a horse or buggy on the alley. I asked about the woman in the white gown and she has been reported by many as well. They are not sure if she is Mrs. Steward or someone else.

Oak Alley Plantation is spellbinding. This antebellum beauty will definitely leave an impression. You can tour the home and grounds, have lunch, shop in the gift shop, and even spend the night on the property. Fans of the paranormal may even encounter a ghost or two. Oak Alley is one of the South's most amazing Historic Haunts.

The amazing photograph of the Lady in Black taken by Plantation visitors seen here in a postcard, notice the difference between the image on the left and the reflection in the mirror on the right.

AMERICA'S MOST HAUNTED HOUSE?

Myrtles Plantation, St. Francisville, Louisiana

The Myrtles Plantation is believed by many to be the most haunted bed and break-fast in the country. I was fortunate enough to investigate here in February 2011 and had many of my own experiences. This wasn't my first trip to the Myrtles. I have visited there several times and had paranormal encounters each time. However, after doing a full overnight investigation I had no doubt in my mind. The Myrtles investigation was one of the most active investigations I've ever had.

History of the Myrtles Plantation

Before we get into the reports of the paranormal activity, we must first know the history and stories of the plantation. The area now known as the Myrtles Plantation was once owned by the Tunica Indians. This area also reportedly contained Indian burial grounds. When the Spanish came to the area they took the land from the Indians and that, reportedly is when a lot of the property's misfortune began.

The story of the first house on this property began with General David Bradford. Bradford, a highly successful attorney fled Pennsylvania when his part in the Whiskey Rebellion of 1794 branded him a trader to the Federal Government when warrants were issued under President George Washington for his arrest. As Washington's troops approached Bradford's home to arrest him he reportedly crashed out a second story window to his horse and road off to the Ohio River. Making his way down the Mississippi to a Spanish area that would later become the Louisiana Territory. There under the jurisdiction from Spain and free from prosecution he purchased 650 acres and began to build a home.

The home was completed in 1796 and he named it Laurel Grove. He lived alone there until 1799 when he was pardoned for his role in the Whiskey Rebellion by John Adams.

Afterwards Bradford moved his wife Elizabeth and 5 children from Pennsylvania to Laurel Grove. Bradford died in 1808. Later one of his law students, Clark Woodruff, married his daughter Sara and moved to the plantation to help manage the property for David's widow Elizabeth. Clark lived here with his wife Sara Matilda and their three children, Cornelia Gale, James, and Mary Octavia.

Clark and Sara had many slaves on the plantation. One in particular was named Chloe. She was a beautiful young woman and the now Judge Woodruff, took an extreme liking to her. She was pulled from her work in the fields and made the house servant to help with the children, cooking, and duties inside the house. She was also brought in by Woodruff to take care of his personal needs.

Eventually the Judge tired of Chloe, especially her one bad habit, she would often eavesdrop on the Judge's closed room conversations. She listened to hear about slave trades and the selling of other slaves, but also reportedly to insure her position in the household and make sure she wouldn't be sent back out to the fields. One day, she got caught and Judge Woodruff was furious. He took Chloe outside to one of the out buildings and had one of his slaves cut off her ear to teach her a lesson. He told her if he caught her doing it again, she would be sent back out to the fields. Or worse, she would hang. Chloe took to wearing a green turban to cover her missing ear.

Chloe wanted to stay in the house, and devised what she thought was a clever plan for doing so. As one of the children's birthdays was approaching she volunteered to make a birthday cake, but planned to put just enough oleander in it to make the family sick. By her reasoning, she would cure them all, nursing them back to health and they would want to keep her in the house. Unfortunately, she misjudged the amount of oleander and made the family deathly ill. Luckily enough, the baby James was already in bed and the Judge was out of town, but Sara Matilda, Cornelia Gale, and Mary Octavia all died from the lethal dose.

Chloe knew she would be killed and started to run away, but was caught by a mixed mob. She confessed and was hung on the grounds. Her body was weighted with rocks and then dumped into the river.

Woodruff remained on the plantation until 1834 and sold the plantation to Ruffin Gray Sterling. Sterling moved in with his wife, Mary Catherine Cobb, and his slaves. They started an extensive remodeling to the home and by the time they were done it was twice the size it had originally been. They needed the room, they had 9 children.

Sterling's wife brought in French craftsmen and spared no expense to create a magnificent building for her and her family. She even changed the name of the place to The Myrtles to reflect the beautiful Crepe Myrtles on the property. Being somewhat superstitious she had crosses put into the stained glass and the key holes of doors installed upside down. Details believed at the time to protect from evil spirits and prevent bad luck from striking the family. She even had items purchased that were built by nuns. This too, she felt, would further protect the Sterlings from bad luck. Unfortunately, five of the Sterling children died at an early age. Sterling died in 1854 and left the plantation to his wife.

In 1865, Mary hired William Winter to help manage the property. He was also a lawyer. (If you ask me, seems like a bad place for those in the legal profession.) He married Mary's daughter Sarah and they had 6 children. One of the Winter's children was three year old Kate. After developing a strange illness the Winter family was so desperate to see her healthy a Voodoo Priestess was reportedly brought in to try and remove her sickness. The Priestess failed and was hanged. Kate, unfortunately, succumbed to Yellow Fever and died.

The hardships for the Winters family did not end though, money was tight and they sold the plantation in 1868. Two years later they were able to buy it back. Their trials weren't over yet. William Winter, being a lawyer had made more than a few enemies throughout the years (in his practice and during his time fighting in the War Between the States). In 1871, William was shot on the front porch by a man suspected to be E. S. Webber. In several accounts Winter came inside and died on the steps in his wife's arms (the 17th step to be precise).

Sarah remained at the Myrtles until her death in 1878, and Mary Cobb stayed here until her death in 1880. Mary's son Stephen inherited the plantation and sold it in 1886. The Myrtles changed hands many times through the 21st century.

Teeta and John Moss have owned the Myrtles and raised their children here for the last several years and have so many experiences of their own. The children's spirits still residing at the house, even interacted with Teeta and John's children when they were still little growing up in the home. The Myrtles Plantation is now an extremely haunted bed and breakfast where you can spend the night and possibly have a paranormal experience of your own.

Haunted Tales of the Myrtles Plantation

As expected there are many ghostly tales surrounding The Myrtles especially with the lengthy history of the property. The first "reported" sighting was in fact made by General David Bradford himself. Bradford claimed to have seen the ghost of a naked Indian girl, a spirit still encountered occasionally to this day. Other reports detail the apparition of a turbaned woman (believed to be Chloe) known to tuck people in at night. In addition, several paranormal reports have been made describing noises and apparitions of children at play as well as a Voodoo priestess chanting over a little girl. Still more reports describe Mr. Winters apparition struggling to get to his wife, as well as sounds of the grand piano playing and crying babies. In all, at least 12 spirits are thought to reside on the property, and many are very active.

I spoke with a former guest who was woken up in the middle of the night by what felt like children jumping up and down on the bed. The guest sat up quickly and the activity stopped. There were no children staying at the bed and breakfast that night and no animals in the building.

My Personal Experiences at the Myrtles

My first visit here was during the day taking the historic tour of the plantation. I was roaming around the grounds and snapping photos of everything. As I got closer to the slave shack I felt this intense sensation of sadness and dread. It got heavier and heavier the closer I got. It was so strong I had to struggle not to cry. As I walked away from the area and went around to the front of the main house the feeling was gone, just as quickly as it had come on. Others who claim to have experienced similar phenomenon attribute it to Chloe trying to let others know she's there.

My best experiences, however, occurred during the formal investigation I executed with my Historic Haunts Investigations equipment. While the rest of my team was unavailable, I did my best to fill their shoes. I was fortunate enough to stay in Judge Woodruff's room. While unpacking the equipment, I looked out the back window towards a bridge leading over to the gazebo and saw what appeared to be a Civil War soldier. He was very misty in appearance and was walking across the bridge before he just disappeared. I frantically tried to grab a camera, but the entity was gone before I could capture it.

With such a "spirited" beginning to the investigation I quickly began to set up (more than a little determined not to miss another opportunity). No sooner had I set up the equipment in the Judge's Room and on the upstairs landing than I heard what sounded like very heavy footfalls coming up the main staircase. It was recorded on the digital recorder, but nothing was captured on the video camera. There are many reports of activity attributed to William Winter or his wife Sarah Matilda, but these sounds were definitely not the sounds of female footsteps.

As the night went on and I started to get tired, I retired to my room. Since I was staying in the Judge's room I made sure to have an IR camera, lap top camera, K2 EMF Meter, Mel Meter, RT-EVP Recorder, and digital recorder all running and pointed towards the bed. This may seem strange, but Chloe's ghost is believed by many to tuck people in at night. I made sure the meters were all in sight of the cameras, and the cameras were all pointing towards me in bed as I settled in.

As I started to lie down I said a few words to Chloe. I told her good night, threw all the blankets to the end of the bed and lay down to sleep. About an hour and a half later something woke me up. When I woke up, the blankets where pulled all the way up to my shoulders and were tucked in all the way around me. I was so excited, Chloe had tucked me in and I had captured it on film! I jumped out of bed to check the IR camera, it was off. I thought. "How in the world could I have forgotten to turn the camera on?" So I went to check the lap top, it was off! I sat there pondering to myself, "why had all the cameras shut off? There was no way I forgot both cameras, besides, why would the plugged in lap top be off?" I powered up the computer, turned the IR back on, and got everything recording again. I threw the blankets to the end of the bed and again went back to sleep. About an hour later, something woke me up yet again. I woke up to the same situation; the blanket was tucked in all the way around me and pulled up to my chin. I jumped out of bed again, but was even more disappointed to discover the IR was off, the lap top was off, and this time the digital recorders were off too!! I rewound the footage on the cameras and there was nothing there.

I said, "Ok Chloe I guess you don't want to be on camera." Hoping to mislead the entity into showing itself I turned everything back on and went back to bed with the blankets almost on the floor. About an hour or so later, it all happened again. I woke up under the blankets, and having made peace with the idea that whatever this entity was it refused to be captured by my equipment on this occasion said, "Ok Chloe, it's getting chilly, I will keep the covers on me this time." I slept like a baby the rest of the night. I never did capture this phenomenon on film or audio, but I did have an amazing experience.

While my cameras didn't work, others have. Several TV shows including Unsolved Mysteries (among others) have reported unusual sounds, movement of furniture, and other unexplainable phenomenon while filming here. Further, while taking a picture of the space between the buildings for the insurance company the current owners captured the transparent image of a slave girl (believed by many to

be Chloe). A National Geographic filming crew confirmed the appearance of the apparition. Whether this is Chloe is a matter of speculation. In fact, many of the details of the stories surrounding the plantation have come under some scrutiny. Historical records and details from the time make it harder to determine what may be Cajun folklore and what may be fact. However, one detail is certain regardless of the

Photo taken by owners and verified by National Geographic Film Crew courtesy of the Myrtles Plantation (above) close up of "Chloe" (top right)

identities of the spirits present, The Myrtles is definitely haunted! I was honored to be able to investigate and feel confident acknowledging (as The Myrtles does) that this plantation is "one of America's Most Haunted Houses".

Close up of the image on the porch

Photo taken by guest with spirit "Chloe" on porch courtesy of the Myrtles Plantation

TIME CAPSULE OF THE SOUTH
McRaven Home, Vicksburg, Mississippi

One of the oldest homes in Vicksburg is also said to be the most haunted house in Mississippi. The McRaven house was built in three different periods. It has been called the "time capsule of the south" and offers an extraordinary look at life in the old south and of the souls who once inhabited it (and may still today).

McRaven's History

The first part of the McRaven house was built in 1797 in Spanish Colonial style by Andrew Glass. It served as a way station for pioneers in route to Nashville. This part of the house is known as the "pioneer section".

In 1836, Sheriff Stephen Howard bought the house and added on the now middle section of the home in an American Empire style. The Sheriff's wife Mary Elizabeth Howard died during child birth in 1836 in the middle bedroom. In 1849, a Greek revival addition was added by John H. Bobb after he purchased the property.

Early in the Civil War, during the Siege of Vicksburg in 1863, a field hospital was set up in the area. These types of field hospitals often saw much death and despair (sometimes this included the residents) and Union forces captured the area of Vicksburg (including the McRaven House). After an altercation with drunken US soldiers who had angered him by plucking some of the flowers from his garden, John Bobb was murdered on the property in 1864. His widow Selina Bobb sold the house to a realtor in 1869. The property sold again in 1882 to William Murray.

In the span of time from 1882-1960, William Murray, his wife Ellen Flynn their daughters Ida and Ella, and their son all died in the house. The house was sold again in 1960 by Annie Murray to the Bradway family who restored McRaven. In 1984 Leyland French purchased McRaven completing further restorations.

McRaven's Ghosts

There are no doubts that Confederate soldiers died during its use as a field hospital and may be responsible for some of the paranormal activity on the grounds. In addition, the house and grounds of the McRaven home were used as a weigh station for Indians in 1831 during the "Trail of Tears". This too might explain some of the paranormal activity believed to spread throughout the house and grounds.

The ghostly legends of McRaven are bolstered further by the five inhabitants who died in the home or on the property, and the murder of past owner John Bobb. In addition there are rumors of Indian burial grounds near the property.

One of the spirits often encountered at McRaven is the wife of Stephen Howard, Mary Elizabeth (who died in childbirth at 15). She is seen in her old bedroom, on the staircase, and in the dining room. She loves to make her presence known by messing with table lamps in the house turning them on and off at will (especially the bedside lap in her room). She has even been known to move things around. People who have actually witnessed her apparition say she is very beautiful. There are also related stories involving Mary's wedding shawl which has been known to emit heat to some who

73

handle it, while others claim it jumps out of their hands!

The ghost of former owner William Murray has been seen on the staircase and his daughter's Ella and Annie are also seen throughout the property skipping, running, and playing as children do. Many have also reported childlike laughter on the property as if they are still playing their favorite games. An American Indian has been reported walking the grounds looking very stern and upset. No doubt an angry victim of his people's forced migration.

Besides seeing full body apparitions on the grounds, people have also reported misty shaped figures which often appear in photos. EVP's (electronic voice phenomenon) have also been captured while people try to communicate with the spirits here.

Guests have even unexpectedly been touched by spirits when no one is around. Employees don't like to close at night because of this. Several ghost hunting groups have explored the property and agree that there isn't anything malicious here; it just gets a little creepy from time to time, especially if you're alone.

The McRaven House and the activity within have drawn interest for years. It has been featured in National Geographic Magazine and LIFE. It has also appeared in television on channels like A&E TV, The Travel Channel, History Channel, and the Discovery Channel.This taste of pre-Civil War Mississippi near Vicksburg is a must see for fans of Historic Haunts, paranormal enthusiasts, and anybody who wants to take a step back in time.

THE BLACK PELICAN
The Black Pelican, Kitty Hawk, North Carolina

The Black Pelican Restaurant

North Carolina's Outer Banks are haunted! This seems to be the consensus from many people I've interviewed in the area. Not surprising, since this outlying area has hosted or witnessed several historic and impactful events, the kind of events that can often leave residual paranormal energies. For starters, this region of the Carolinas has seen pirates come and go and was just a few miles south of the famous ironclad duel between the USS Monitor and the CSS Virginia (formerly the USS Merrimack). Additionally, many unfortunate sailors had to contend with the Outer Banks shorelines and inlets, a primary reason for the large number of lighthouses and lifesaving stations. At one time in the late 1800's, the North Carolina coast boasted seven such stations. However, one of the more interesting locations to me has always been Kitty Hawk.

Kitty Hawk's Station Six

Kitty Hawk Lifesaving Station, or "Station Six" as it was called, was one of seven stations erected along the Outer Banks of the North Carolina coast. It was built in 1874 from Cypress shipped from the mainland. It provided a sturdy and secure base of operations for a crew of six surfman and one keeper to maintain a wary eye on the restless Atlantic shoreline. These men tirelessly risked their lives rescuing unfortunates who fell prey to the dangerous waters of the Outer Banks. Appropriately, the station itself would prove to be just as hardy as its bold and courageous lifesavers, surviving two moves from the rising sea levels and erosion, and countless Nor'easters. In fact, the Kitty Hawk Lifesaving building and US Weather Station may be the only "Gilded Age" structure in this area to have survived these violent storms for over 100 years! Still in use over 130 years after its construction, but no longer a lifesaving station, today it hosts the Black Pelican Restaurant, a delicious native sea food eatery and local hotspot. Visitors here can enjoy a great meal and learn the history of this building collected in old photos and memorabilia on its walls. It's a rich history with epic flights, rugged surfmen, and murder.

The Deadly Rivalry at Station Six

In 1884, the surfmen of Station Six were under the orders of Captain James Hobbs. His reputation preceded him. He was known as a strict disciplinarian, he demanded respect and had little tolerance for disobedience. When he gave orders they were to be obeyed without question. Unfortunately, one brash and arrogant surfman was assigned to the station and had other ideas. T.L. Daniels was a handsome and cocky young life-saver who didn't like taking orders and who felt a strong dislike for Hobbs. Their mutual dislike and distrust led to many encounters. Then in July of 1884, a serious argument erupted between Hobbs and Daniels, during which Daniels insulted Hobb's wife. This was apparently the final straw for Hobbs. He reached for his revolver and shot Daniels in the head, killing him, in front of his wife and the lifesaving crew. The blood reportedly splattered on the occupants as well as the furniture and floors. After cleaning up the mess, the Station Six crew took the surfman's body in one of their boats and buried it at sea. The lack of nearby law enforcement and the testimony of the crew allowed Hobbs to be cleared of any wrongdoing.

Station Six as it looked in 1900
courtesy of U.S. Coast Guard

Happier Days for Station Six

In 1900, a remarkable turn of events would allow Station Six and its surfmen to play a pivotal part in history. A letter arrived in Kitty Hawk made out to "the man in charge of the surrounding territory, especially to learn if there are any sand hills." This letter originated in Dayton, Ohio from one Mr. Wilbur Wright. The letter left post mistress Addie Tate a little uncertain about the best man to deliver it too. She would pass the letter on to her husband William J. Tate. Tate was a remarkable man of action who served as assistant post master, and a member of the nearby Lifesaving Station. William was familiar with earlier publicized efforts made by others to glide. He notified the Weather Station head, and prepared a most impressive response. He not only responded with detailed descriptions and numerous sketches of the area, but he also extended hospitality to the Wrights and described the amazing hospitality of the people of the area. His letter - along with a favorable report of the winds of the Outer Banks from Kitty Hawk weather station chief Joseph Dosher -was the reason the Wright Brothers chose Kitty Hawk to begin their own gliding experiments.

Wilbur Wright arrived on Tate's front door on the morning of September 13th, 1900. Tate and his family would welcome the Wrights into their home and form a long lasting friendship. In fact, the brothers began assembling their first glider in the front yard of the Tate home, even stitching the glider's wing fabric together with Mrs. Tate's sewing machine. The Wrights would return each year to test gliders from the sandy dunes of Kitty Hawk and nearby Kill Devil Hills. Each year Tate (and his family) would assist, or when they could not, Tate would enlist the help of his cousin and co-workers from the nearby Lifesaving Station.

Finally, on Dec. 17th, 1903, the Wright brothers succeeded in accomplishing the first flight of a motorized, heavier-than-air flying machine. Orville Wright would come into the Kitty Hawk Lifesaving Station to send the famous telegraph announcing their successful flights to the world. The surfmen were indispensable to this flight, taking historic pictures, aiding as always in assembly and serving as flight crew for the Wright Flyer. William Tate was a big part of this success and would remain an avid aviation enthusiast for the rest of his life, even confirming and helping select the site for the monument to this historic flight on its 25th anniversary.

Early photo of the Tate's and the post office (right) courtesy of U.S. Coast Guard

Captain Tate and the Legend of the Black Pelican

To say William Tate had a knack for helping people is an understatement, he was cited an amazing number of times for saving lives and property, eventually being promoted to light keeper at Currituck Sound. Tate was aided no doubt, by his keen observation skills and his uncanny knack for noticing something that might be important. A testament of this was not only his many rescues, but his careful observation and chronicling of a rather unique member of his crew, the Black Pelican.

The albatross or pelican had long held a mythic status with most mariners. Their appearance typically helped seafarers and others identify and avoid bad weather. Still, a Black Pelican was an even rarer thing, and as Captain Tate chronicled, and the crew of Station Six soon learned, these dark birds would prove to be a invaluable asset to their lifesaving efforts.

One day some of the surf patrol spotted a black pelican circling the shore during a terrible storm with little to no visibility. The bird kept circling one particular area which caught the nervous attention of the crew. The life savers went over to the area where the bird was circling, and discovered a ship in distress. They came to the ship's rescue with the help of the black pelican. If it hadn't been for that bird, they never would have spotted the ship. From then on, whenever the men would see this rare bird they would pay strict attention. The bird would hover frequently near the station with an alert posture and weary glance. "The Black Pelican served as an omen of impending disaster and crucial rescue needs. Effortlessly, the bird guided the men through blinding storms and turbulent waters to the sinking vessel and struggling survivors." Captain Tate wasn't the only one to chronicle the efforts of these open seas watchdogs". In 1927, a Greek tanker named Kyzikes was struck in a horrendous storm. Some of the men rescued from that storm recorded in their journals how they saw a strange looking bird, a black pelican, just before they were rescued. The pelican skimmed the water's surface and continued circling the passengers until help arrived. Some passengers went on to say that they thought the bird was the only reason they were saved from the storm.

With the closing of the station, the bird seemed to vanish. In fact, the pelican population has become endangered and risked disappearing altogether. Protective measures from government-funded projects and conservationist groups have helped bring the pelicans back from the brink. Interestingly enough, modern sightings of the Black Pelican have been occurring frequently around the former Lifesaving Station. Sailors, fishermen, as well as Coast Guard members have reported seeing this mystery bird again, a haunting presence during inclement weather. But, the bird is not the only haunting presence which seems to have reappeared near the former Station Six.

The Paranormal Black Pelican

A mysterious male presence is felt and seen inside the restaurant. Employees and patrons of the Black Pelican have described a mischievous spirit in the place. One that frequently moves furniture and items in the bar, turns off electrical devices, and brushes against staff and diners alike. While my husband and I enjoyed a wonderful lunch there, our waitress shared the story of the blood stain that was on the office floor. She said that before carpet was put down, there was a blood stain on the floor that no one could get up. They put carpet over it and eventually a filing cabinet on the carpet to hide the stain because it seems to keep seeping through as if newly made. The office and carpeted area are located near the exact spot in the building where Captain Hobbs shot and killed surfman Daniels. In fact, most paranormal accounts made by those who have seen the restaurant's spirit describe a man matching Daniel's description.

Surfman Daniels is apparently not the only spirit present on site, however. There has also been a different man occasionally seen walking around the outside of the restaurant, on the decks and stairs. Some people have described him as a sea Captain. Others believe it to be the ghost of Captain Tate, still on the job. There has even been some speculation that the increased encounters with this spirit might coincide with the frequent sightings of the black pelican birds and the instances of dangerous and unsafe weather.

If you are in Kitty Hawk, besides all the amazing history in the area, look to the skies. On a stormy day perhaps you'll see a suspicious black bird or an observant sea captain. If the weather is beautiful (and hopefully it is), make sure you stop by and have a fantastic meal at the Black Pelican, maybe one of their ghostly residents will literally pull up a chair to join you.

THE BROWN MOUNTAIN LIGHTS

North Carolina

(Can be viewed from various locations near Morganton and Linville)

Would you be scared by an eerie floating light in the darkness? How about several? While these questions sometimes come up with paranormal accounts of orbs, another intriguing version might be the "Brown Mountain Lights"

The Lights are Reported and Explained?

One of the earliest modern day accounts of the Brown Mountain Lights dates back to September 1913, when a journalist from the Charlotte Daily Observer reported on the subject. The lights were seen above the horizon by a fisherman. He reported seeing red colored lights floating above the horizon on a nightly basis.

Many geological surveyors and the Smithsonian investigated and concluded that the lights were misidentified train or automobile lights, city lights, fires or stationary lights. However, in the 1922, just after the surveyor's reports went public, a massive flood hit and some of the roads, bridges, and railroads were flooded or washed away, and all electrical power was lost. The lights, inexplicably, continued to be seen.

Since then the lights have continued to be appear, garnering numerous investigations and drawing the attention of scientists, authors, paranormal groups and tv shows (they were featured on an X-Files episode). The only details that seem certain is that they are best viewed from September through early November and that there are a great many legends and superstitions that surround them.

The Legends of the Lights

One of the earliest reports of the mysterious lights was in the year 1200 by the Catawba and Cherokee Indians. Indian lore states that hundreds of years ago the Cherokee and Catawba Indians had a terrible battle on the ridge of the mountain. Many of the Indian warriors died and their bodies were left behind. That night when word got back to the rest of the tribes, the women went out with torches searching for the husbands, sons, and fathers who fought and died on that bloody day. The Indians believed the sad event was so powerful that it still haunts the area and is the cause of the lights seen above the mountain ridge.

Another legend involving the brown mountain lights involves a plantation owner who lived here in the 1800's. He was very kind to his slaves and they all respected him. One night the plantation owner went out to hunt and never returned. One of the slaves went out with a lantern to search for him. He never found the plantation owner and he too disappeared. Some locals believe it is his lantern still seen today searching. However, this doesn't explain the reported sightings since the 1200's.

A third legend details the gruesome murder of a wife and child and their secret graves on Brown Mountain. The lights reportedly appeared over the graves and illu-

79

minated the area, leading the locals to discover their bodies. The murderer reportedly escaped, never to be seen again, unlike the frequently appearing lights.

Shedding Light on the Speculation

Some people believe the brown mountain lights are UFOs flying along the ridge. Others believe they are energy or gas bubbles being released from the earth. Additional theories abound, involving everything from paranormal entities to interdimensional beings, "little people", fairies, or conscious beings of energy that occupy the mountain.

My Own Enlightening Experiences

Despite the many theories about Brown Mountain, there is something out there and I have seen the lights myself. Standing at the Brown Mountain Overlook watching along the ridge, I saw the mysterious lights start to appear just above the ridge. Having lived in the Carolinas, I have witnessed multiple lights in the sky on numerous occasions and at different times of the year. Without fail, every time I've been in the vicinity of Brown Mountain like many other spectators and groups, I've seen them!

Whether you believe the lights are the supernatural manifestations of the Indian maidens, UFOs, fairies, earth's energy, or other causes there is definitely something occurring along the ridge. There have even been sporadic reports since the 1770's of unexplained sounds in the area (although these reports are overshadowed by the consistently recurring light show). With all the inexplicable lights and sounds in the area, you have to admit this is one mysterious Historic Haunt.

HELEN'S BRIDGE

Helen's Bridge, Asheville, North Carolina

Paranormal investigation is all about bridging the gap between the living and those who have passed on. In many cases we investigate a location or circumstance where "bridging the gap" literally involves a bridge. Usually these are tragic situations centered around the collapse of the bridge, but not always. One of the more interesting and unique bridge haunts I've investigated was Helen's Bridge in Asheville North Carolina.

Helen's Bridge

The Bridge's History and the Local Legends

The bridge now known as Helen's Bridge was built in 1909 for easy access to Zealandia Mansion on Beaucatcher Mountain. At the time it was known as Zealandia Bridge and was a highly regarded piece of architecture and construction. It was designed by R. S. Smith the field architect for the beautiful Biltmore House. Even its construction from quarried stones set it apart from other mountain bridges and access ways. The legend surrounding the bridge and its haunting, however, are what really kept this Blue Ridge beauty in the public consciousness.

I spoke with an elderly gentleman a few years ago who grew up on Beaucatcher Mountain and had lived there all his life. He was familiar with the legend about the local woman who had built a home on Zealandia. He told me the story he knew since childhood about Helen's Bridge (and the version that popped up repeatedly during my research).

One night the lady of the house, Helen, was home alone with her young daughter. The youngster was playing in the bedroom alone. It was a cold night so the fireplaces were burning throughout the home to keep the place nice and warm. The child was playing in its bedroom with the door closed and setting on the floor near the fireplace when hot ambers popped from the fireplace on to the child's nightgown and caught the rug on fire as well. The fire spread quickly and the child was crying and screaming. When Helen came to the door, it was locked. She couldn't get in. Smoke and flames were coming from the room and Helen could not save her child. The child perished in the blaze and Helen thought it was entirely her fault. She was so distraught over the loss she went to the top of the bridge and hung herself from it.

Helen's Ghost and the Bridge

Many people have told me that when you drive up the mountain and approach the bridge or up to the mansion and call out to Helen she will appear to you in some form. She is most often described as a sad glowing figure wandering the mountains in a

81

long gown, and those who have encountered her claim to have problems with the electrical systems in their vehicles. The more Helen manifests herself to the curious, the more intense the problems. Paranormal reports describe everything from dead batteries (extreme sighting) to the more commonly reported problems with electric locks, doors, and windows.

Of course, I decided I needed to go check this out myself. I went up there with another investigator and we walked around the area of the bridge. I snapped a few photos and said a few words to Helen in case she was there listening. We then went up to the mansion and took a few photos there. We were sitting in the car and about to leave when I had the overwhelming urge to take one more photo. While sitting in the passenger seat I took another photo of the mansion, and as I did I saw a woman out of the corner of my eye go around the front of the car. I turned thinking my fellow investigator had gotten out of the car. Instead I discovered that my cohort had the same surprised look on her face, she had seen the woman too!

We investigated more thoroughly, but decided to leave when we turned up no other evidence. As we left we were talking about the sighting and wondering if maybe Helen was letting us know she was there. We decided to grab some lunch (since it was that time) and look through the photos on the camera. When we got to the restaurant and got out of the car we couldn't get the electric doors to lock. It took five tries to get them to lock. This car had never had problems before this. We shook our heads wondering if it could be Helen doing it. Were we now one of several people who reported trouble with automatic locks and windows after experiencing something by the bridge?

We had lunch, looked through the photos and found nothing. When we returned home, the locks still weren't working right. About a week later the car was still suffering issues with the locks, so we figured we'd go back up to the area one more time and ask Helen nicely to leave the car alone. We did just that and the locks worked perfectly after that. We had no other personal experiences near the bridge that day.

The strange phenomenon at Helen's Bridge is still going on. I got an email just a few weeks ago about problems with someone's car windows. I told them to go back up there and ask her nicely. It worked, their windows are fine now.

While Helen is the main entity encountered here there have been other reports of activity associated with the bridge. People have reported dark and monstrous things coming from the woods, and incidents with victims being slapped, hit, and scratched. Other reports detail apparitions, orbs, and other unusual occurrences. Locals believe this may be tied to the Indian burial grounds discovered nearby in the 1940's. They claim the activity increased around the bridge once the graves were disturbed.

If you do go up to Helen's Bridge please respect the privacy and no trespassing signs, and ask Helen politely to leave your car alone. If not you might have to make a second trip up the mountain or call a tow truck. I never recommend provoking spirits, and in the case of this Historic Haunt, if you do you might find yourself walking home!

THE GHOST OF THE DWARVEN JESTER AND THE CASTLE

Joseph Johnson House, Beaufort, South Carolina

Joseph Johnson House

What are a castle and a court without a jester? Hard to say, and not a debate we often have in America. In the early days of North America's exploration one jester, a dwarf, reportedly came to this country and never left. While he may not have filled the history books with his exploits in life, he has certainly drawn notoriety after his death.

Jean Ribault and Gauche

According to history, Jean Ribault, a Huguenot and explorer led an expedition to the New World in 1562 that saw his land in present-day South Carolina. Ribault was thought to have brought a jester with him, a dwarf named Gauche. The dwarf was outfitted as a typical jester with hose stockings, pointed shoes, colorful blouse, and bells on his pointed hat. This impish character was thought to be belligerent and mischievous. It has been speculated that he may have been one of Ribault's South Carolina colonists, and that he may have met his demise in a vicious three-way battle, through cannibalism, or being impaled on a spike. Details of this unusual character remain sketchy until the late 1800's.

Joseph Johnson's Castle

Dr. Joseph Fickling Johnson began constructing a house with Italian style influences in 1850 on property he owned in Beaufort South Carolina. It was located near a great bend in the Beaufort River amid giant live oaks and rich gardens of azaleas and camellias. This grand almost medieval looking house became better known to the locals as "The Castle". Perhaps because it sported all the amenities that most people couldn't even think of affording. During the Civil War the unfinished residence was confiscated by the Federalist troops to be used as Military Hospital #6. One of the out buildings served as a morgue during the Castle's turn as a hospital.

When the war ended Dr. Johnson, like only a handful of southerners, was able to get the house back, but only after paying $2,000 in taxes. After the war Johnson was able to get this stylish landmark completed. The home remained in the Johnson family until 1981.

It is rumored that there are many unmarked graves on the property, most likely a product of the lives that were lost during the Civil War. The remains of a smaller,

83

more jovial Frenchman are also rumored to be somewhere nearby, and the death and turmoil of the Civil War is believed to have "woken up" this long gone spirit.

The Haunted Castle and the Ghost of Gauche

Stories of spirits and ghosts on the property started early on in the life of The Castle. The gardeners claim to have seen apparitions soon after the house was completed and the doctor himself claimed to have seen the spirit of Gauche walking outside the house.

Joseph's daughter Lily claimed to have paranormal encounters as a child there as well. She told stories of having tea parties as a little girl and a little elf like creature would come to the party in bright colored clothing with bells on his hat. She allegedly reported experiencing this several times. When she spoke of him she said that he told her his name was Gauche.

At first Lily had to develop a way to communicate with the dwarf who would rap on the tables. Over time they developed a spectral Morse code of sorts that allowed Gauche to communicate with them, and them to understand his early archaic French. During these communications Gauche became infamous as a rough and mischievous character who swore frequently. House guests reported his activity to be more like a poltergeist and he reportedly liked to decorate the Castle's windows with red hand prints. They also mentioned an unusual feature of the house located on the top level. Apparently in one of the bedroom closets is a small door that connects inexplicably to the bedroom closet next to it. Regardless, residents after the Johnson's have described this place as having a "creepy air" about it (especially the basement).

Gauche's spirit apparently still haunts the grounds. Witnesses have reported a dwarf like apparition appearing and the sound of bells jingling. People blame Gauche for anything mischievous that seems to take place, including opening and closing doors, moving objects, even furniture being out of place.

Besides the little Frenchman, Joseph Johnson's apparition has been seen here walking the grounds. He has also been seen walking through his gardens, especially around the azaleas and the two olive trees he planted from the Holy Land.

Joseph Johnson's castle has been called "one of the great houses of the South Carolina coast". It is thought to be one of the most photographed houses in America and the oldest and most haunted site in South Carolina. This amazing building and its lush and scenic surroundings seem to make a ghostly dwarf want to keep coming back. With all the natural beauty on property I don't blame the doctor either for wanting to return to his very own Historic Haunt.

THE GHOSTLY EXCHANGE AND THE PARANORMAL POSTMAN

Old Exchange and Provost Dungeon, Charleston, South Carolin

The Old Exchange and Provost Dungeon

They say imitation is the sincerest form of flattery. In 1670 a group of colonists left Britain and settled here at Charles Towne hoping to create their own idyllic version of restoration England. While the new world was rich in the types of commodities that made trade flourish (rice, indigo, cotton) it also drew the unwanted attention of pirates, Indians, Spanish invaders and wild animals. To protect themselves, the residents of Charles Towne built a set of fortified walls that surrounded the city. In fact, Charles Towne was the only British walled city in North America. In addition, a half-moon battery (semicircular fortification) was built projecting the sea wall. Behind it were the council chamber and jail. Charles Towne continued to prosper and drew the attention of pirates like Stede Bonnet and Blackbeard. Stede Bonnet was captured and held with his men in this jail in 1718 before being hung. Blackbeard fared much better as he plundered the prosperous city and even blockaded the harbor.

Prosperous Charles Towne

Charles Towne continued to thrive and prosper with shipping continuing to increase exponentially. Charles Towne became one of England's busiest and wealthiest trading partners. A brisk slave trade began in Charles Towne, and helped the port to continue to grow quickly. It became obvious that a large exchange and customs house was needed to accommodate the expanded shipping business. The sea wall was lowered in 1767, and the area was filled to create an open air exchange directly on the water that could handle the traffic of the busy port. Construction began on the Royal Exchange and Customs House in 1767 and was completed in 1771 by the Horlbeck brothers. In the main level was an open arcade and trading area, on the second floor an elegant assembly room and city and customs offices were built. The ground level contained cellars used for storing goods. In its heyday three hundred ships could be seen in its port. It was the South's largest port, and all ships from large sailing vessels to barges and canoes had to send a representative to the customs house to pay the required duties.

85

The Charles Towne Tea Party & Independence Hall of South Carolina

Steep duties and tariffs on goods and services in the new world led to angry Colonists who felt they were being unjustly taxed without representation. While this outrage led to the dumping of tea in Boston Harbor (the famed Boston Tea Party) in Charles Towne the tea was seized, stored (in the cellar of the Exchange Building) and later sold to fund the patriot cause. The tide was turning against the British. In 1774, South Carolinians assembled in the Great Hall of the Exchange and elected delegates to the Continental Congress. Charles Towne produced four signers of the Declaration of Independence, and on March 28, 1776 South Carolina declared its self independent from Great Britain from the steps of the Exchange. This led to its nickname as îthe Independence Hall of South Carolinaî.

The British Were Coming, the British Were Coming

British troops laid siege to Charles Towne for 42 days in 1780. They gained the upper hand and marched in to Charles Towne taking over the Exchange Building. Leading citizens of Charles Towne (including signers of the Declaration of Independence) were rounded up and imprisoned in the cellar under the Exchange. The area set aside for this purpose was called The Provost. The prisoners endured cramped quarters, contaminated food, disease, and death. Many of these early American citizens were left to drown with rising water levels and when dead, were left chained beside the living to be food for rats. American patriot Colonial Isaac Hayne was imprisoned in the Exchange before his execution in a small room off the Great Hall (which is today named after him). After the Revolution the British would leave and in 1783 Charles Towne would be incorporated as the city of Charleston with the Exchange serving as City Hall and Customs Office.

The Exchange Moves On

In 1788 the Great Hall of the Exchange Building witnessed the historic vote that led to South Carolina becoming the 8th state to ratify the US Constitution. President George Washington would be the toast of the town in 1791 with a weeklong stay in Charleston that included many events held in the Great Hall. The building was sold to the Federal Government in 1818 and used as a Post Office in 1896. The US Light House Service would occupy the building in 1898; in 1913 the building was saved from becoming a gas station by the Daughters of the American Revolution in a tremendous preservation effort. Today it serves as their meeting place and a wonderful historic education site.

Plentiful Paranormal

I have visited the Old Exchange and Provost Dungeon numerous times, and without fail I have had paranormal experiences every time I've visited. During my first visit there I was touring the dungeon. I was getting ready to enter the area where the tour starts when I saw the chains that surround the exhibit slowly start to sway. I didn't feel a breeze and as heavy as those chains were, I don't believe that it would have been possible for an air vent to move them. As the tour guide approached our tour

The Ghostly Exchange and the Paranormal Postman

group the chains immediately stopped. I thought this was rather odd and couldn't wait to examine the area and do the tour. Later, while on the tour I approached the chains that were swinging earlier and realized they were much heavier than I had previously thought. There were no air vents or drafty areas around to have caused a breeze. Further, if the chains had been swinging from normal means they would have slowed to a stop, not stopped abruptly as if someone or something stopped them.

As the tour guide continued we were introduced to a few of the Dungeon's past prisoners. The Provost dungeon has manikins and animatronics to tell stories in the dungeon. They play an audio of the prisoner's stories while you look around the area and watch them move. As we were at the second exhibit area and I was listening to the audio of the prisoners telling their side of the story, I felt as if someone were behind me. I turned and looked thinking there was someone trying to see over me, and there was no one there. I turned back around and was still listening to the tale when all of the sudden I felt a hand on my shoulder. I turned to see who it was and as before there was no one there. My mom, who was beside and in front of me looked a little spooked and said, "Someone just touched me!" I said, "Me too!"

We turned back to the display a little bewildered when we were both suddenly pushed as though someone were trying to squeeze through and past us. I looked at my mom and she looked at me, we both just shook our heads stunned.

We moved on to the next display wondering who or what we had just encountered. The audio started and we couldn't help, but look around waiting for something to happen again. We glanced back at the area where we had been pushed and we both saw one of the manikins move. It was a manikin and not an animatronic. I took a photo and captured a very strange light anomaly in the area where we had just been.

After the tour we asked the guide about the animatronics and the manikins and she confirmed which ones moved and which ones didn't. I then asked the guide, "So, who is still down here?" She looked surprised and said, "Did he touch you?" The guide went on to tell us that apparently several people have reportedly been touched by this unseen visitor tagging along on the tours. In addition, voices are also heard along with the sound of footsteps following you, and mysterious cold spots are felt throughout the basement. There have been no reports of anyone getting hurt, but several of people getting freaked out.

We finished our chat with the guide and returned to the main floor of the building where you can tour on your own. I was by myself when I came across a reconstruction of the old Post Master's office. For some reason, I

Captured image of the Post Master's Ghost (above) Closeup (right)

was very intrigued by it and felt I should take photos. There was no one around me in any direction and no manikins or animatronics in the area. When I returned home from the trip and had the pictures developed, I learned I had captured an apparition of a man who appears to be a postal worker in one of my photos. He was transparent, but you could tell he was an older man, with balding hair, and a slight belly.

At the time, a friend of mine volunteered at The Exchange and I sent him the photo. His reply was, "WOW!" He had heard of the ghost of the old post master and people had reported seeing him, but he had never seen a photo of him. Apparently the image in my photo matched the description of the Post Master.

I have had many similar experiences on different occasions and in different areas at Charleston's Old Exchange Building. It seems as though this building never fails me when it comes to paranormal experiences. I have always had some sort of ghostly activity occur when visiting here. The activity I encounter is the same as that which is so often reported here. The ghosts of the upper areas of the Exchange seem to be generally related to the many events and activities hosted or housed there and the duties performed there. In this case, in the upper area apparitions of the Post Master and polite society members of the Revolutionary era are most often reported. The lower levels of the building (including the Provost Dungeon) seem to have a much more menacing paranormal presence. Many witnesses and guides describe encountering disembodied crying and moaning, and others describe being pushed or choked. In other cases, tourists approach what they think is a staff member in period costume (which is the normal mode of dress for the tours) only to watch the "staff member" vanish before their eyes. Whether exploring the upper areas of the Old Exchange Building or the lower, it would seem that this Historic Haunt is full of ghostly encounters, from top to bottom.

ZOE AND THE PARANORMAL POOCH
Poogan's Porch, Charleston, SC

Poogan's Porch

Stories of the paranormal sometimes ruffle feathers or in some cases fur. Poogan's Porch, a Charleston institution, is not only the home of amazing Low Country /Southern Cuisine, it's also the residence of the restaurant's furry little name sake, a little dog named Poogan. His spirit is reportedly still in the neighborhood, one of a few encountered at this historic Queen Street establishment.

The History of Zoe & Poogan

The building that would later become Poogan's Porch was built in 1888 as a private residence. One of the former residents was Zoe St. Amand who lived here with her sister Elizabeth (Liz). Zoe and Liz rented the bottom half of the house and Zoe was a teacher at Craft's House School, which was just down the street. Both ladies were spinsters and never married. Zoe outlived her sister by 9 years. She spent most of her adult life here at 72 Queen Street. Zoe died in 1974 but after her death she apparently returned to the house. Zoe died alone, but many people think she may have returned to be surrounded by people and activities. Zoe is one of the most talked about ghosts in Charleston.

The family that owned the house after Zoe lived here had a dog who loved to sleep on the porch and watch people walk by. His name was Poogan and he was a West Highland white terrier. A neighborhood fixture, he had accepted table scraps and back scratches from every family on the block. All the locals who walked by knew Poogan.

When the new owners bought the place in 1976 they wanted to turn it into a restaurant, but they noticed one thing. The former owners left Poogan behind. The new owners figured that since Poogan had pretty much claimed the porch; they would call the restaurant Poogan's Porch and the name stuck. As the restaurant took off Poogan greeted customers from his perch on the porch and became a Charleston institution. Poogan passed away of natural causes in 1979, but his spirit apparently never left the house or his front porch.

89

My Experiences with Poogan and Zoe

During my first visit to the restaurant I hadn't heard any of the stories about the place being haunted. My family and I had stopped in just to have lunch. While we were sitting at the table and talking about what we wanted to do in Charleston, I suddenly felt something brush up against my leg. I have a cat at home and my first thought was that it felt like an animal rubbing against me. I looked under the table and there was nothing there. Then I thought maybe my mom (who was sitting next to me) had brushed my leg with her foot. Just as I began to ask her if she had bumped me, she looked at me and said, "What?" I gave her a puzzled look and she told me that she thought I had just bumped her leg and wanted to know what I wanted. We both looked under the table and around the room and saw nothing.

Later our waiter brought out our delicious looking food and we started chatting about lunch. All of the sudden we both felt it again. We both got up from our chairs and looked under the table. If other patrons saw us they probably thought we were nuts. At about that time, our waiter came out, stopped and looked at us peering under the table, and asked, "Is Poogan wanting attention again?" We both went "Huh?!" He then began to explain the story of Poogan and how he never left after his death. His spirit frequently rubs up against people wanting attention and to be petted. Our waiter said it happens on a regular basis. People also reportedly see him sleeping on the front porch a lot in his usual spot. Our waited continued, "He is completely harmless; he just wants a little love."

We finished our lunch and paid the bill, then decided to go upstairs and check out the rest of the building. Maybe Poogan would be upstairs too? As we walked up the stairs we both felt like there was someone else with us. We chalked it up to being an old and unleveled staircase and continued up. As we reached the top of the stairs we were surprised to be hit with hot air. We figured this was heat from the kitchen and we knew heat (in general) rises, so we decided that was why it was so much warmer upstairs. Still, such a small and localized spot of warmth was almost too extreme. However, we didn't give it too much thought as we walked around the upstairs and went into the front room that overlooks Queen Street. Suddenly we were hit with a massive burst of cold air. It felt like an ice box in there. The AC wasn't running, it wasn't cold outside and the rest of the upstairs was hot, so why was this one room so cold?

We came out of the room and a waitress was heading downstairs as we were rubbing our arms trying to get warm. The waitress saw this and replied, "Oh, Zoe must be in there again." Then she continued down the stairs. We followed her down the steps eager to find out more, but we didn't get the chance. The restaurant had gotten busier and we didn't want to interrupt her work.

On our way out we paid our respects to Poogan (who's buried here) and went on our way exploring Charleston. We decided we would do a ghost tour that night since our encounter at Poogan's Porch was so intriguing.

We got checked in for the tour, they gave us a brief history of things and we headed to the first stop. What do you know? The first stop was Poogan's Porch!

The guide started telling us the story about the friendly terrier that we'd heard earlier. As he did this I looked up at one of the upstairs windows. To my surprise I spotted a woman in a black dress with her hair pinned up tight on her head staring out the window. I must have looked a little slack-jawed, because the guide stopped his story and came over to me. He turned and looked at the house, then turned back to me and asked, "What did you see?" I described to him what I had seen and he looked shocked. He pulled a book out of his bag and showed me a picture, asking, "Was it her?" I replied, "It was." The picture he showed me was Zoe!

Like me many people have reported seeing her ghost walking around (before disappearing) and feeling extreme hot or cold spots in the house when her spirit has been present. People have also heard footsteps and report being touched.

Sometimes Zoe gets upset with employees and visitors who are not respectful. She has been known to knock things over and spill glasses to make a point, and has been experienced in the kitchen making pots and pans crash inexplicably. She has never harmed anyone, just wants a little recognition and respect, and like Poogan a little attention.

This Historic Haunt is full of history, spirits of both kinds, and impeccable food drawing rave reviews from celebrities like Paul Newman, Jim Carrey, Jodie Foster, Joe Namath, and Hugh Grant, (among others). It is a must while in Charleston, one of the nation's top 5 most haunted cities. I can't wait to go back there, maybe next time I'll bring a bone.

THE BELL WITCH
John Bell Farm, Adams, Tennessee

There are few supernatural stories in American history as well-known as that of Tennessee's Bell Witch. Like many of these stories the details seem to vary with each telling. Regardless of the details of the version you hear, the tale and the Bell Witch have become a major part of Tennessee's personality and history (the story was even included in a Federal Government's guide book for the state). Among those interested in the paranormal the Bell Witch encounters are some of the most disturbing and long lasting in history (human interactions with the spirit date all the way back to 1817). So how much of it is true and how much is folklore? Let's get into the history and you can decide for yourself.

The History of an American Haunting

John Bell was a farmer from North Carolina who settled in Tennessee in 1804 with his family. He bought 320 acres along the Red River and built his home, grew his crops, and raised his family peacefully for thirteen years. The family grew and became prosperous. That is until the summer of 1817, when everything changed.

The family started seeing strange animals in the woods at night, hearing knocking sounds on the walls, windows, and doors outside the house. Eventually the sounds moved inside the house, the family encountered sounds of chains rattling and being dragged across the floor, the sounds of someone gulping or being choked, along with the sounds of stones being dropped on wooden planks. In some cases these stones seemed to be falling from the sky, because the family could never discover where the stones were coming from.

The Bell family was terrified and didn't know what to do. Most people at that time had their whole lives intertwined with their land and couldn't afford to just pack up and move out. John was also a deacon in the Red River Baptist Church and may have feared what the congregation and locals might say. The family kept all the problems to themselves for about a year, and then John decided to confide in his neighbor James Johnson. Bell trusted James and invited James and his wife to come stay at his house to see if they experienced the same terrifying things the Bell family had been suffering through.

James and his wife stayed for a few nights and witnessed the strange occurrences that John Bell had described for themselves. James convinced John that others should be told about what was going on.

Soon word spread like wild fire and people from all around came to hear and witness the unseen force at the Bell's farm. As time went on, whatever it was that was tormenting the family gained enough strength to have a voice. Many people asked the entity what it was, there were a few different answers, but there was one reoccurring answer, that it was the witch of Kate Batts. Later, the entity became known as Kate, the "Bell's Witch".

Kate Batts was known in the community as a mean old neighbor of John Bell. Perhaps because she believed he cheated her on a land purchase. On her death bed,

92

Kate reportedly swore that she would haunt John Bell and his descendants.

The Kate entity told many she had two reasons for haunting the family. One was to kill John (she would never give her reasons), the other was to keep John's daughter Betsy from marrying a young man, a neighboring boy named Joshua Gardner. Betsy and John received the worst of the witch who tortured and tormented the members of the Bell family daily for the next three years. Betsy had her hair pulled and was pinched, scratched, stuck with pins, and even beaten. John became weaker and weaker and at times began suffering through spells of feeling like his throat was swelling shut. The family started hearing Kate cussing at John and making hideous threats when he was choking, as if she were in a fit of rage trying to kill him. She also made his facial muscles twitch and jerk in painful and uncomfortable ways.

Kate was getting a lot of attention from nearby regions and drawing crowds. As more people gathered she seemed to get stronger and bolder. Although unseen, she manifested more and interacted with the curious. Her claims to be a witch seemed more believable as she began to act less like a "haunt" and more like something else (some consider her to be an early example of a poltergeist). She not only seemed extraordinarily intelligent on a variety of topics including the Bible, she also seemed to know hidden details of people's past and future (including the curiosity seekers), and could literally manifest in two different places at the same time (sometimes miles apart from each other). Among the curious witnesses was reportedly the future president Andrew Jackson. He stayed here in 1817 with some of his troops and was quoted as saying, "I had rather face the entire British Army than spend another night with the Bell Witch."

Eventually on December 20, 1820 Kate got her wish. John -who was believed to be poisoned by Kate-died (a strange vial was reportedly found in the medicine cabinet and when a drop was given to a cat on property, killed it immediately). Kate took full credit for the death and the details of the poisoning (she even reportedly sang loud and obnoxious drinking songs throughout John's burial until all the guests had left). Betsy was afraid she might be the next one to die. A short while after her father's death and at her wit's end she broke off her engagement with Joshua in hopes that Kate would leave them all alone.

Pleased, Kate bid the family and everyone else goodbye, but promised to return in seven years. She did return in 1828 for a few short weeks. She came to the house of John Bell Jr. and told him there was a reason she killed his father, but she wouldn't tell him why. She also reportedly revealed to him through long talks, details about the past, present, and future, and made predictions (including reportedly the Civil War). She then said she would return in 107 years, and again she kept her promise and coming back in 1935.

By this time the large number of people traveling great distances and coming and going from the Bell's house had left it in pretty bad shape. It was torn down in the late 1800's for safety reasons, and a new cabin was reconstructed. Many of the items from the original home were salvaged and preserved along with other artifacts in a nearby cave (now called the Historic Bell Witch Cave). After her reported return to the area in 1935, many locals feel that she never left and now inhabits the cave.

Paranormal Activity Still Experienced

People have been reporting activity attributed to Kate ever since then. From choking sounds, voices, cussing, strange animals appearing, and even stones that appear to be falling from the sky. Others described problems with their cameras near the cave (pictures of the cave often show up black), and instances of people being "pushed" in the cave (especially towards the cave exit as if something wants them to leave). There have also been stories of those who have visited the cave and brought the "curse" of the Bell Witch back with them. These people described repeatedly and randomly finding items around their homes impossibly broken, glass shattered, and other items destroyed or damaged for some time after their visit. Could all this activity really still be going on or are people just keeping the legend alive or caught up in the superstition?

I have spoken with a few people who have visited John Bell's farm and said they experienced some strange things (like the stones falling from nowhere). There has been some speculation that the Bell Witch might be associated with Indian spirits from the nearby "Trail of Tears". Other stories claim that locals in the Adam's area were dabbling in Black Magic during the time of John Bell.

If you visit the area it will surprise you. It is full of farm land and rolling green hills, and boasts great canoeing and kayaking on the Red River. For fans of the paranormal and Historic Haunts, it is a very interesting legend that has been around for over 200 years. If you have the courage to visit the Bell Witch Cave (miles deep and 40 miles north of Nashville) you can opt to take a candle light ghost tour. If you do you might discover the truth of the story for yourself.

THE SPIRIT OF A FOUNDING FATHER
Monticello, Charlottesville, Virginia

"All men are created equal..." and have a right to "life, liberty, and the pursuit of happiness." Famous and eloquent words authored by one of the most fascinating and accomplished of our founding fathers, Thomas Jefferson. Do these same values apply to the afterlife? The lives and deaths of our founding fathers are the stuff of history books, yet even among this amazing group of men Jefferson was unique. Still, no dialogue about Jefferson can be complete without mentioning the amazing residence that inspired and nurtured the man himself, his beloved Monticello.
"...all my wishes end, where I hope my days will end, at Monticello."
*~Thomas Jefferson 1787 ***

The Little Mountain

Postcard from Monticello

Monticello, an International Landmark and American Icon, began life as Monticello Mountain, a 5,000 acre plantation that was inherited by Jefferson after the death of his father Peter Jefferson in 1764. Monticello was an Italian word meaning "little mountain", and it was this mountaintop that Jefferson began leveling in 1768 to build his dream residence. He based his designs on concepts of neoclassical architecture, which he had taught himself. Monticello's first inception was as a two-story, eight room house, which Jefferson had mostly completed by 1784. However, in 1796, Jefferson - inspired by houses he'd seen in Paris during his time as a diplomat in France - started to transform Monticello into a three-story, 21 room structure. He would consider this building his "essay in architecture" and his efforts would span 40 years of construction, design, and remodeling. To accomplish his goals he would have the upper story removed, extend the east front, create a new second level, and incorporate design elements from famous buildings of antiquity. Among Monticello's unique features is a dome over the west front, the first on an American house, and the first "dumbwaiter" in use in the U.S. The house also boasted open-air living spaces, L-shaped terraces, sky lights, lush gardens and a book room which housed one of the largest private collections (which Jefferson would later donate to become the heart of the Library of Congress). This structure housed Jefferson's family, the 150 slaves in his service, and special areas for pursuits in woodworking, nail making, carpentry, tobacco, farming, astronomy, archaeology, botany and many many others.

Taken from the Monticello Brochure

95

An Historic Eyewitness

Monticello not only provided a place to house Jefferson and apply his theories on agriculture, technology and research, it also witnessed many noteworthy times in his life and in our country. In 1772 Thomas married Martha Wayles Skelton, a 23 year old widow; later in 1772 Martha would give birth to their first daughter who they named Martha. Mary, their second daughter would be born in 1778. Jefferson's wife Martha died in 1782 and their daughter Mary died in 1804 and they are both buried on the property along with Thomas himself.

As a statesman, Jefferson served in the Virginia House of Delegates in 1777, and was elected Governor of the State in 1779. In 1781, the British attempted to capture Jefferson and other members of the Virginia government at Monticello and they failed. Jefferson served as a diplomat to France from 1784-1789. He became Vice President to John Adams in 1796, and was elected President of the United States in 1801. He was re-elected for a second term in 1804.

While living at Monticello, Jefferson was a lawyer, a member of the House of Burgesses, a member of the Continental Congress, and the first Secretary of State under George Washington. Monticello also inspired him to write. Among the noteworthy pieces he penned were: A Summary View of the Rights of British America, the Declaration of Independence, and the Statute of Virginia for Religious Freedom, as well as many papers and treatises on various topics of interest to him. His literary and scholarly pursuits would even inspire him to found the University of Virginia while retired to Monticello.

Thomas Jefferson lived a long and productive life at Monticello with so many more details there isn't enough space in this book to cover all of them. He died at Monticello on July 4th, 1826, coincidentally the 50th anniversary of the adoption of the Declaration of Independence, the same day his dear friend John Adams died. Unfortunately, when Jefferson died the plantation was not profitable, and despite his best efforts debt forced his family to sell the land, home contents, and the enslaved workers to attempt to pay off the debt.

Monticello's Benefactors

Jefferson's family sold the property in 1831, to Dr. James Barclay. He in turn, sold it to a Jewish naval officer, Uriah Phillips Levy in 1834. The Levy family would prove to be spectacular caretakers for the better part of 90 years. Several members of the family (great admirers of Jefferson) invested great sums of money, not only in maintenance of the property, but also in renovation and restoration. In 1923, the Thomas Jefferson Foundation purchased Monticello from the Levy family. The foundation still owns and oversees the upkeep and tours of the museum, gardens and grounds. Monticello is the only house in America designated as a United Nations World Heritage Site.

Paranormal Monticello and my Own Experiences

Needless to say with all the events that took place here it is very likely there is at least some residual energy still lingering. With no prior knowledge of the place being haunted before my visit here, I soon found out for myself that Monticello was full of paranormal activity. I was fortunate enough after going on the main tour downstairs to receive a private tour of the second floor and the dome room. That's where I first encountered the ghostly activity. There were only three of us on the tour, including the tour guide. While walking down the hall I noticed large holes in several of the doors close to the floor. As I pointed them out inquiring to the tour guide, I felt something brush up against my leg. The guide said they were doors for Jefferson's cats so they could come and go as they pleased. I asked him if they still did and he in return asked me, "Why? Did one rub against your leg?" Apparently according to our guide the cats or at least one of them is still haunting the old house and taking advantage of the "cat doors". Many people have claimed to feel a cat rubbing against them.

We continued the tour of the second floor and I heard someone whistling. I didn't dwell on it much thinking it was probably a worker in the house whistling away. As we made our way towards the door of the room it seemed to be coming from, it continued. Just as we began to enter the room, the whistling stopped. I later found out (after asking many questions) that Mr. Jefferson often whistled while he did his work and many workers and tourists have experienced this to this day. Most reports in similar fashion described hearing a tune until entering the room it was coming from, then it stops (the room the visitors entered was otherwise empty of all but them)! By this point I was not surprised to learn that the three of us were the only people in the house.

Another commonly reported paranormal occurrence here is the sighting of a young boy. Many people have reported seeing a transparent young boy around the age of ten wearing a tricorn hat looking out a second floor window. No one seems to know who he is for sure, but if they look up and wave at him he will wave back or nod his head, then disappear.

An Unexpected Ghostly Photo Op?

While happily reliving my trip to Monticello reviewing my pictures from the building and grounds, sometime later, something caught my eye. A picture taken of me in the dome room showed a man in a formal outfit (perhaps a servant) in the window to my left. There were no paintings or images on the walls to cause a reflection in the window, nor were there any areas outside that could have reflected the image or re-enactors or others in period outfits present. In addition, the three of us on the tour were all wearing casual clothes and none of us bore any likeness to the man in the window. Apparently I had gained a paranormal souvenir of my visit to this amazing property and another unique story for my book. Overall, Monticello is an amazing place to visit rich in history and haunted by several, including one of my ancestors, President Thomas Jefferson. Rest in peace cousin Thomas.

Me visiting Monticello (top)
Close up of "spirit" in the window (right)

GHOSTS AT COLONIAL WILLIAMSBURG... A CAPITOL IDEA

The Capitol Building, Colonial Williamsburg, Virginia

Who speaks for independence? In the formative days of America, it was clearly the voices of the gentlemen of Virginia. Gathered as they often were at the colony's "capitol" in Williamsburg; these brave men debated and framed concepts and ideas that would later initiate American Independence. They spoke of rising tensions between the monarchy and the colonists, and ultimately instructed the Virginia delegation to forward the question of freedom at Philadelphia's Continental Congress. As lofty and solid as their ideals were, so too were the

The Capitol Building

foundations and peaks of the building where they convened, a tall brick building that seemed to dominate Williamsburg's east end, the Capitol Building.

An Historic American Foundation is Laid

After the Jamestown Statehouse was destroyed by fire (for the third time) in 1698, the House of Burgess made the decision to move the Virginia Colony's government to Middle Plantation, soon after renamed Williamsburg. The decision was also made on May 18th, 1699 to build the first American structure which would have the word iCapitolî applied to it. Since the legislature had temporarily taken residence at the College of William and Mary's Wren building; they looked to contractor Henry Cary to help with their new structure. Cary was already finishing work on the Wren building when they chose him to devise their new capitol. Cary came up with a simple and efficient concept for the structure. It was to be a two story "H" shaped building, in actuality it was two buildings connected by an arcade. Each building was 75ft by 25ft. The first floor of the west building was used for the General Court and the first floor of the east was used by the House of Burgesses. Stairs on one side led to the Council Chambers, a lobby, and the Council Clerk's office, on the other side stairs led to conference rooms, and other offices. Cray also included a six sided cupola on top of the building to fly the flag. The west wing was completed in 1703, but the entire building wasn't finished until November 1705.

The "Capitol" Undergoes Some Changes

The Capitol building visitors see today is substantially the same as Cary's original. Cary's building had no fireplaces or chimneys, but they were added in 1723. This proved to be a big mistake, the building burnt down on January 30th, 1747, leaving only the foundation and a few walls.

In March, Governor William Gooch ordered another Capitol to be built. John Blair laid a foundation brick on April 1st, 1751 for a redesigned structure that didn't resemble Cary's original. It was completed by 1753 and the house got down to business. On May 29th, 1765, Patrick Henry gave his "Caesar Brutus" speech against the Stamp Act. As the tensions grew between the people of the colonies and mother England; other early American founders met, debated and framed legislation. Among these famous men were George Washington, George Mason, George Wythe, Richard Henry Lee, Thomas Jefferson, and many others.

Blair's building was last used as a Capitol on December 24th, 1779 when the General Assembly adjourned to reconvene in May 1780, in Richmond, the new Capitol of Virginia. The building then saw many new uses including a law school, a military hospital, a grammar school, and female academy. The west wing was sold in 1793 for its bricks and demolished. The building's east wing burned down in 1823. In 1881 the last above ground traces of the building were removed.

Cary's Capitol Reborn

When Dr. W.A.R. Goodwin started his restoration project in Williamsburg, he had excellent documentation of Cary's original design of the Capitol building. The decision was made to refurbish the new capitol with the aid of well preserved 18th century records. Cary's design was deemed more interesting. On February 24, 1934, this new version of Virginia's old Capitol Building was dedicated with a ceremonial meeting of the general assembly (they still meet there once a year).

Despite its current status as a reconstruction of an early Capitol, the foundation this building rests on has seen its fair share of history. Guests of Colonial Williamsburg may come here hoping to discover Virginia's living history, but may be surprised to find a touch of the non-living still trying to make history.

Ghosts of the Capitol

Supernatural activity at Colonial Williamsburg is fairly common. It has spawned many lantern lit tours and candlelight discussions. Like many paranormal groups before me, I found myself drawn to the Capitol for historic and haunted reasons. While I've had many telling experiences of my own; once again I thought the best reference on paranormal activity at the capitol might be the people who experience them repeatedly, the many wonderful employees and volunteers of Williamsburg.

One of the most popular and enduring ghost stories relayed to me about the Capitol involves Independence Day. It has been reported that at the stroke of midnight on July 4th, the spirits of Patrick Henry, and our revolutionary leaders assemble again. I haven't been able to experience this particular patriotic manifestation for myself, nor have any of my contacts at Colonial Williamsburg. However, when my contacts and I have discussed ghosts, it's a different set of stories I hear from them.

One of the amazing workers at Colonial Williamsburg is historic interpreter Michael Pfeifer. He has encountered many times the spirit of a little girl who he has affectionately nicknamed "sweetheart". He has heard her call out "Mommy?" and she has been known to follow him around the building from time to time. He informed me that many people have reported sensing her presence, though she seems to refrain from manifesting herself visually. She has been known to open and close shutters on the windows. I don't know if she is just trying to help whoever has closing duties, or if she is trying to keep them there so she has company. Michael is even convinced that sweetheart has followed him home, as he has experienced some of the same phenomenon in his own place after returning home from working at the Capitol.

Another good friend of mine, Mark Couvillon, has worked for the Colonial Williamsburg Foundation for 22 years, and like Michael has had a few experiences of his own. He described one to me that occurred in February 2012. This is his experience as he related it to me:

"I was unlocking the Capitol building around 8am in the morning before the rest of the staff arrived. I was on the phone to security telling them I was opening the building. I saw a person in blue walk down the steps into the courtroom. I thought it was one of the maintenance people (as they wear blue) and I followed the person into the courtroom. When I walked in no one was there! I checked all the doors in the courtroom to see if someone could have left and they were still locked and bolted! Not sure what I saw, but I definitely saw someone walk down the stairs and into the room. Mike Pfeifer said he has heard people talk about seeing a woman in blue at the Capitol on numerous occasions and I think that is who I saw."

In fact, the lady in blue has been seen by an extraordinary number of people over the years. I too had an experience while attending a friend's performance of "Cry Witch" (a reenactment of the witchcraft trial of Grace Sherwood). I was sitting on the high bench next to his Excellency when we both saw something float across the balcony above. It was a dark blue color but looked as if it was holding a white handkerchief. There was no one on the balcony, but my friend and I both saw this woman. It was like someone was walking the entire length of the balcony with a handkerchief in their hand while holding the rail. One popular rumor among those working at Colonial Williamsburg is that the lady in blue was a former tour guide who loved her job so much, that after her death she never left.

Like this mysterious employee, Colonial Williamsburg holds a very special place in my heart, being related to many of the important people of Williamsburg's past, and having lived there myself. I have collected Williamsburg memorabilia for years. While living there I chanced upon an estate sale and bought a collection of old photos from the historic area dating around the 1940's. When I got them home and started going through them, one in particular caught my eye. The picture showed an older woman that seemed to match some of the reports I'd collected standing in a doorway of the Capitol. She was wearing a dress, but it's hard to tell the color since the photo is black and white. She was holding a white handkerchief. Coincidence? Could this be who still haunts the halls of the Capitol? We may never know, but I'll keep going back to this great Historic Haunt and hope I someday find out!

Interior shot of the Capitol

PELHAM'S GHOSTLY PENNIES
Public Gaol, Colonial Williamsburg, Virginia

A History of Incarceration

Crime and punishment are very serious matters. In 1699, when Middle Plantation (now known as Williamsburg in honor of King William III) became the capital of Virginia, the need for a facility for those that broke the law became increasingly apparent. In 1701, the Virginia General Assembly ordered a brick prison to be built. It was known as the public gaol (pronounced jail from the old French word "gaole"). Contractor Henry Cary was given the job of building the gaol (he was also tasked with completing the Capital Building, the Governor's Palace, and the Wren Building at the College of William and Mary).

*The Public Gaol
Colonial Williamsburg*

In May of 1704, the gaol was ready with two cells and was located on Nicholson Street. It would hold debtors, runaway slaves, and from time to time the mentally ill. During the Revolutionary War it also housed Tories, spies, military prisoners, deserters, and traitors. The building was not meant for long-term imprisonment, it was used instead to hold people awaiting trial in the General Court at the Capital Building just up the hill, or for convicts awaiting their sentences of branding, whipping or hanging. Nevertheless, in 1711 two more cells were added because space was needed for debtors and others. In 1722, the keeper's quarters were extended and an exterior courtyard was added.

The building provided a suitable means of housing law breakers with little to distinguish it, though there were a few celebrity prisoners here. In 1718, 15 of Blackbeard's henchmen were held here just before their hangings. Another well known resident of the gaol was Henry Hamilton, lieutenant governor of British Detroit, captured in 1779. These "guests' of Virginia's penal system infamous or not, were tended by gaol keepers John Redwood, William Wyatt and John Lane respectively.

Peter Pelham was the last keeper of the gaol from 1771-1779 and is still the most remembered. Besides being the gaol keeper, Pelham was also the organist at Bruton Parish Church and taught ladies to play the spinet and harpsichord.

Pelham and his wife, Ann, had 14 children, some of which died during infancy, but at least five of them grew up at the gaol, and one of them was even born there. In 1780, after Pelham's turn at keeper, the Public Gaol became a county facility and served as such until 1910. It was later restored and dedicated to the Colonial Williamsburg Foundation in 1936.

VIRGINIA

Paranormal Pennies From Heaven?

Having lived in Colonial Williamsburg, and being lucky enough to be a descendent of the Randolph's of early Colonial Virginia; I have many ghostly tales to tell. Truth be told I could write an entire book on the topic, however, I'd rather share the experiences of a dear friend of mine. His name is Michael Pfeifer and he has worked as an historic site interpreter for the Colonial Williamsburg Foundation for over 8 years. Here is his story:

"This story is about a true event that happened to me at one of the sites that I work at- The Public Gaol. The Gaol (pronounced jail) has two of the original cells (completed in 1704), but the rest is reconstructed. Mr. Peter Pelham was the Keeper of the Public Gaol during the 1770's. There have been stories about noises, footsteps, and sightings before, so we jokingly say that Mr. Pelham is still keeping an eye on the Gaol.????

One day in early spring 2006, another interpreter and I were scheduled to work at the Gaol. Since there were only 2 of us, we would take turns interpreting the site. One of us would interpret for an hour while the other took a break, and then we would switch. I was interpreting first, so my co-worker went to get a cup of coffee at the break room in the Capital. It was still early, and no guests had arrived yet. That means that I was entirely alone. Or was I?!?????

While opening the Gaol site, I noticed that there was something wrong with the modern central air system. It was extremely stuffy inside the Gaoler's house. There was no air movement, and it was way too hot inside. First, I called Work Control to make them aware of the situation. Then I decided that I would open the back door leading to the exercise yard and original cells outside and then come back and open the front door of the house. Perhaps that would let some air flow through and move out some of the "dead air". I walked through the Gaoler's house and opened the back door as planned. I then started back to the front of the house. While I was walking through the hall (parlor) I heard what sounded like a coin hit the floor behind me. I stopped and turned around. Sure enough, there was a Lincoln head penny lying on the floor behind me. Again I turned around to find another Lincoln head penny lying on the floor. Still unaware of anything odd, I bent over to pick it up. Again I heard a coin hit the ground behind me. I bent down to pick it up. Again another penny hit the ground behind me. The pennies continued to drop in just this fashion for what seemed like several minutes. ????

I did begin to think something funny was going on. My first thought was that I had a hole in my pocket, or change that had stuck to my clothes somehow, so I checked. No holes in either pocket and no clinging change. Besides that, I NEVER carry change in my pockets. The pennies weren't mine. Then I began to suspect a co-worker was playing tricks on me. I searched the whole house and found no-one. Since there are only two doors and I could see them both from where I stood, I am sure that no one had entered. Finally I said, 'Well Mr. Pelham, I'm glad you took a liking to me, but if you're going to drop money on me could you make it a Virginia half-penny, or a shilling or two? Even a 20 would be nice.'????

Then the pennies stopped dropping. I picked up the last one and put it in my pocket with the rest. I could hear my colleague coming down the path from the Capital, so I opened the front door and went out on the front steps to wait for him. When he got there, he noticed I had a confused look on my face and he said, "What?!?"????

I said, "Clayton, the strangest thing just happened to me!" and I began to tell him the story and describe my efforts to remove the "dead air". While I was talking, the front door slammed shut and something came flying out from inside hitting me in the chest. He said, "What was that?" I said, "It was probably a penny." I looked at the ground and it WAS a penny. I picked it up and put it in my pocket.????

I went home with 35 pennies in my pocket that day. They were all modern pennies with assorted dates. There were no wheat pennies. I did not notice if they fell heads up or tails up.????

I shared the story with all my co-workers - with the benefit of Clayton as a witness to the end of it - and they were all amazed. Some couldn't believe it, and some just plain got freaked out. They all swore that they hadn't done it. They said that if it had been them they would have claimed it. It would be too good of a prank to go unclaimed.????

So where did the pennies come from? Did Peter Pelham or another spirit decide to make them known to me that day? I don't know. I have worked at the same site many times since then, and nothing else has happened to me."

Michael's experiences of paranormal activity at the Public Gaol are not unique. There have been a large number of paranormal incidents reported there. Most reports describe activity like Michael's. Some describe seeing full body apparitions peering out the windows (as Michael mentioned in the early parts of his story). Other reports describe footsteps, noises, or the ghosts of two women heard in animated conversation on the second floor of the jailer's quarters.

Colonial Williamsburg's Public Gaol seems to have no shortage of paranormal residents and activity. While many of these haunts may be intelligent, attempting to communicate - some in the paranormal field believe spirits often attempt to communicate by dropping or manipulating small change - others seem to be just residual. Unlike Mr. Pelham, these "residual haunts" merely replay some discussion, passage, or activity without the benefit of giving us their "two cents"

If you are intrigued by the sites of Colonial Williamsburg and the paranormal activity here, make a point after visiting the gaol, of walking up the hill to the Capital Building. That is where the next chapter will take you and perhaps another experience awaits (it did for Michael). This entire town is full of Historic Haunts.

THE ASYLUM AND ITS PARANORMAL PATIENTS

Trans-Alleghany Lunatic Asylum,
Weston, West Virginia

A mind is a terrible thing to waste they say. In the paranormal field there is strong belief in ties between the mind and residual psychic impressions or residual haunts. Some may chalk these types of things up to "our mind playing tricks on us", but sometimes repeated evidence occurs to the contrary. This is the case with the Trans Alleghany Lunatic Asylum. A frequently, investigated paranormal site that is considered by some to be one of the most active in the US.

Weston Hospital
courtesy of Wikimedia Commons

An Active History of "Crazy" Conditions

Also known in its past as Weston Lunatic Asylum and Weston State Hospital, the asylum was in use from 1864 until 1994. Because the hospitals main building is the largest hand-cut stone masonry building in the U.S.; it was added as a National Historic Landmark in 1990. The hospital was originally authorized by the Virginia General Assembly in the early 1850's as the Trans Alleghany Lunatic Asylum and construction was started in 1858. Construction began with prison laborers and skilled stone masons brought over from Ireland and Germany.

Construction was briefly interrupted by the start of the Civil War in 1861, but resumed in 1862 with the acceptance of West Virginia as a U.S. State that same year. At that time it was renamed the West Virginia Hospital for the Insane. The facility admitted its first patients in 1864, but construction continued into 1881.

It was intended to be self-sufficient with its own farm, dairy, waterworks, and cemetery. Ultimately, it totaled 666 acres in all (a coincidental number that may raise an eyebrow to some in the paranormal field). It was renamed Weston State Hospital in 1913.

The hospital was designed to hold 250 patients in solitude, but in 1880 it already housed 717. By 1938 the patient count was up to 1661, and by 1949 the count was over 1800. It peaked in the 1950's with over 2400 patients. Obviously overcrowding was a major issue. The hospital originally intended for the mentally ill became a place to dump epileptics, alcoholics, drug addicts, and those deemed "mental defectives". The hospital was plagued by poor sanitation, insufficient furniture, lighting and heating. These conditions resulted in the mistreatment of many patients.

The hospital saw some relief by the 1980's when changes in the treatment of mental

104

illness helped reduce its population. The decision was made to build a new psychiatric facility elsewhere in the state. Patients were moved to other facilities and the mistreatment and overcrowding finally stopped. There were several attempts to repurpose the facility before it was auctioned off in 2007.

At that time Joe Jordan bought the property for $1.5 million and the building and grounds are even now undergoing major renovations to help fund the restoration projects and preserve the facility the old hospital is now open for day time historic tours to experience what 19th and 20th century life was like in a mental hospital. They also do ghost tours at night to show visitors the other side of the hospital, and more intense overnight ghost hunts.

An Asylum for Paranormal Activity

Weston's Asylum has achieved something of a cult status among those interested in the paranormal. Even the appearance of the building suggests it. Hand carved images of humans, animals, and gargoyles, peer out from the gothic building's stone face. An ominous two hundred foot clock tower rises eerily from the mist of daybreak and twilight. An appropriate setting perhaps for the horrors that happened inside. The asylum documented deaths well into the thousands from leeching, electroshock, lobotomies, and mistreatment and abuse from the staff. There were even numerous cases of murder between patients, most horrendous and grizzly crimes. With all of this in its past it's no surprise that there might be reports of paranormal activity in the hospital's historic wards and treatment rooms.

Many visitors to the hospital have reported hearing sobbing coming from certain rooms as if patients were still there. Drawn to these areas by the noise, the curious found only empty rooms. Other witnesses have reported seeing a patient curled up in a corner wearing a white hospital gown. They believe it is a woman, even though they haven't seen her face. She has been seen in a few different locations.

Some visitors to the old hospital have seen misty forms appear right before their eyes only to dissipate as the visitor got close. People also report hearing voices in different locations of the building. The rattling of chains has also been heard as if someone were shackled to a wall or a bed trying to get loose.

There are numerous other îsymptomsî of a haunting at this facility that read like a patient's chart. Tour guides and visitors describe ghostly touches and odors, sounds of crying, screaming, laughter, and moaning. Apparitions of men and women walking down hallways are often seen, and gurneys have been known to roll up and down hallways apparently of their own volition. These types of activity have drawn the attention of paranormal groups and televised ghost hunting programs. Many have recorded evidence on heat seeking cameras and sound recording equipment.

The Trans Allegany Lunatic Asylum is an imposing structure. It is an important lesson to us about the mentally ill and caring for our fellow man. Whether you experience something paranormal there or not it is still worth a visit while in the area. Perhaps connecting with a presence at the facility can put even a skeptics mind (and maybe that of a ghostly resident) at ease? One thing is certain though hospitals, prisons, battleships, and other historic structures are all part of our countries history and unpleasant or not deserve to be preserved.

THE EERIE INMATES OF WEST VIRGINIA PENITENTIARY

West Virginia State Penitentiary, Moundsville, West Virginia

There are many paranormal cases that involve spirits who are unable to pass on, prisoners on this plane of existence. Every once in a while there is a historic site which is markedly different from most of the others. The West Virginia State Penitentiary is one of those and raises questions about what happens when the souls trapped here in life are now trapped here in death.

postcard West Virginia Penitentiary

The Penitentiary's Back Story

After an inmate escape in 1865 forced West Virginia legislators to look at constructing a state prison, acreage in Moundsville was purchased and planning began. A gothic revival style of architecture was chosen to mirror the northern Illinois Penitentiary in Joliet and to suggest to incoming prisoners - through its large looming walls and dark appearance - the misery yet to come.

Construction on the main areas of West Virginia State Penitentiary started in 1867 and was completed with prison labor in 1876. Work began afterwards on the secondary facilities.

To keep the prison running and mostly self-sufficient, there were a few industries established within the prison walls using inmate laborers. There was a carpentry shop, bakery, stone yard, paint shop, brickyard, blacksmith, tailor, and a hospital. The prison even had a coal mine about a mile down the street which saved them thousands of dollars every year on energy bills.

Education was even provided for the inmates in hopes of rehabilitating them. In the beginning, the prison's conditions were acceptable, it was clean, and it wasn't over populated. In addition, the food was actually decent (according to inmates reports). Unfortunately, by the 1920's the prison started to decline and over population began. They decided to expand the prison and attempt to stem the beginning of overpopulation before it got out of hand. That worked for a while. Eventually the situation grew

106

The Eerie Inmates of West Virginia Penitentiary

worse, and new unflattering details of the jail emerged. It became evident something would need to be done about West Virginia's State Pen.

Among the stories to emerge over the years were the 36 homicides in the prison and 94 executions from 1899 till 1959, 85 of them were hangings. The last hanging turned macabre when the inmate didn't strangle to death, but was instead decapitated! Because of this the prison decided that hangings were inhumane and the electric chair should be brought in.

On October 8th, 1929 R.D. Wall was brutally murdered by three other inmates for "snitching." The culprits used dull objects as shivs and brutally beat and stabbed Wall till he finally bled to death. As time went on it became obvious too that the security of the prison wasn't what it should be. The cell doors had been picked so many times it was fairly easy to get out of the jail cells. It was becoming known as a Con's Prison. It was even listed on the U.S. Department of Justice's Top Ten Most Violent Correctional Facilities list.

In November 1979, 15 inmates escaped, and then on January 1st, 1986 a riot broke out. With serious overcrowding issues and lack of efficient guards, it was extremely easy for 20 inmates to start the riot. Unfortunately for them, the rioters didn't really have a plan, just a list of demands about changing conditions at the penitentiary. The standoff ended up being a two day event and three inmates wound up dead. The prisoners for all their reasons really didn't accomplish anything. Within nine years of the riot, the prison closed down (1995). It just wasn't doing its job. Poor security, overcrowding, and unsanitary conditions were all reasons that disease spread throughout the prison. These were all cited as reasons for its closure.

Incidents of the Paranormal at the Pen

The cruel and unusual conditions at West Virginia State Penitentiary might explain why the prison is haunted today. Several former inmates are reportedly still haunting their cells. Numerous reports of hushed voices and the sounds of whispers are heard coming from the cell blocks, but when investigated, they stop. It's almost as if the otherworldly inmates were planning an escape. These reports are nothing new; guards at the facility were reporting unusual occurrences as early as the 1930's!

These occurrences continue to this day. Cell doors are often heard slowly creaking open or slamming shut, a phenomenon that has even been captured on video. In this case there are no air sources to explain the door's sudden movement. Further, lights go on and off of their own accord and cold spots are often encountered. When people are touring the building they also hear the sounds of heavy footsteps behind them. When they turn to see who is there they find nothing but empty space.

But perhaps the most startling and frequent paranormal experience at the prison is the shadow figures seen moving and captured in photos. People have often claimed to catch a glimpse of something out of the corner of their eye. When they turn to see what's causing it there's nothing there. Even worse, sometimes they turn to see what's there and they spy a shadow of what appears to be a large man staring at them. The prison guards referred to these shadows as "phantom inmates"! The guards also described one "shadow man" in particular that wandered the premises.

These phantoms and shadows as well as the other frequently encounter activity have earned this penitentiary a reputation as one of the most haunted prisons in the US.

Indeed, several paranormal themed television shows have filmed here over the last few years. Most of these have captured startling and similar evidence of paranormal activity at the Moundsville facility, especially of the shadow figures that turn up frequently on their equipment.

For fans of the paranormal or just history, the prison is now open for historic tours by day and haunted tours by night. Many visitors have said that night fall is always the creepiest at the prison and that you never know who might be lurking around the corner watching you. Is it your shadow moving or something else?

ABOUT THE AUTHOR

Jamie Roush Pearce

Jamie was born in St. Petersburg, Florida. After several unusual encounters at historic sites as a child, Jamie developed a passion for history and the paranormal. She began to research and investigate paranormal sites and stories. She established Historic Haunts Investigations in 2004 to display her research and findings, and provide an outlet where others could share their stories.

She continued her studies in Parapsychology under noted authority in the field Loyd Auerbach. She has gone on to be featured on the cable tv show *Most Terrifying Places in America* and has been proudly featured in several newspaper articles. To this day she continues researching the paranormal, counts several note-worthies in the field as peers and friends, and has even been present at the taping of several shows by famous televised ghost hunting groups.

Jamie was happy with the warm welcome her first book **Historic Haunts** received (now on it's third printing) and has eagerly been working on the sequels. She has been asked to write an ongoing column for the Florida Times Union, and has been a contributor to Jacksonville Magazine as well as other Florida publications. She continues to post the evidence of her investigations and research of the paranormal through her website **www.historic-haunts.net** and with her team **Historic Haunts Investigations.** She lives in Florida with her husband Deric, her living cat Griffin and the spirit of her deceased kitty Cosmo. She has a soft spot for Coca Cola and old Vincent Price movies.

Made in the USA
Columbia, SC
26 September 2022

67975140R00061